U.S. VETERANS
IN THE WORKFORCE

U.S. VETERANS
IN THE WORKFORCE

Why the *7* percent are
America's Greatest Asset

MIKE SCHINDLER
Founder and CEO of Operation Military Family

elevate

Praise for *U.S. Veterans in the Workforce*

For leaders who wish to create a competitive advantage in their fields — be it business, industry, education, non-profits, healthcare or the like — *U.S. Veterans in the Workforce* is not only a must read, it is a must understand. Mike Schindler captures the value-stream that veterans represent in today's workforce with a comprehension that is more informed and in-depth than anything I have encountered to date.

Schindler, himself a veteran and now successful CEO and author, takes the focus off of veterans who are broken or wounded, (a group that certainly deserves society's care and attention, but not one in which the majority of today's veterans fall), and places it with great clarity on the attributes that today's main-stream veterans bring to the private sector.

U.S. Veterans in the Workforce describes the qualities, character and traits that veterans acquire as a result of their service. As I read, I asked myself, "Who would not want employees who 'have learned to work efficiently and effectively under pressure, can manage crisis, are able to win hearts and minds and adapt quickly? Who would not want employees who bring with them the soft skills such as punctuality, work ethic, effort, energy, passion and preparation? Who would not want employees who bring with them $125,000 in federal funding to support their training?'"

Veterans, as Schindler details so well, are not America's problem; they are the solution.

John Andrews
Captain, United States Navy Retired
Former executive for City of Norfolk tasked with Veteran Workforce
Development for the Hampton Roads Region

U.S. Veterans in the Workforce: Why the 7 Percent are America's Greatest Asset is a wonderful tribute to the best of America's values and strengths as found in its veterans. I recommend this book to anyone seeking to understand the modern-day veteran's experiences and challenges, both during active duty and during re-entry into the civilian world of work and higher education. One of those values is "Grit"— increasingly understood today as a key ingredient for successfully navigating our complex workplace and competitive higher education landscape.

College admissions professionals have long looked for personal markers of Grit, such as "productive follow-through," when assessing the qualifications of applicants for admission to selective universities. Mike Schindler correctly hones in on these qualities as part of the returning veteran's success profile, rightfully highlighting their unique experiences and ability to contribute meaningfully to their future workplaces and universities after service to their country.

John F. Swiney, Ph.D.
Special Assistant to the CFO/Vice President
Business and Financial Affairs
Central Washington University

A must-read for HR and College Recruiters.

Bob Dees
Major General, U.S. Army, Retired
Former VP for Military Outreach, Liberty University
Author of *Resilience Trilogy*

U.S. Veterans in the Workforce by Mike Schindler is an important piece, with a unique relevance as it relates to the integration of the marketplace and principles learned through military service. In today's workforce, we're finding more and more companies focused on a "narrow" career path – an inch wide – in a "silo'd" approach. Yet, through military service, we're developing leaders holistically, which means they become more and more valuable in the marketplace as future leaders who can see the big picture.

Jeff Rogers
Chairman & CEO, OneAccord

U.S. Veterans in the Workforce is a rich collection of inspirational achievements about the men and women who have served our country with honor and are now ready to enrich our civilian ranks. As I read this book, I felt the struggles and perseverance of those who transitioned from military to civilian life.

Too often, our veterans must overcome the negative stereotypes placed on them due to a lack of understanding by non-military personnel. I truly believe that Schindler's book can create a Vet-Strong culture in our higher education institutions and corporations by exemplifying the strong leadership foundation and solution-minded characteristics of our veterans. Bravo!

Dr. Jean Hernandez
President, Edmonds Community College

U.S. Veterans in the Workforce showcases the resolve and talent we have in our states just waiting to be tapped. Veterans are the best hire any employer can make!

Lourdes E. Alvarado Ramos (Alfie)
Washington State Director of Department of Veterans Affairs

Editorial Work: Anna McHargue
Cover Design: Aaron Snethen
Interior Design: Aaron Snethen

Paperback ISBN-13: 9781943425952
eBook ISBN-13: 9781943425969
Library of Congress: 2016942579

The events mentioned in this book are actual events, but in some cases the names have been changed to retain the anonymity of those involved. **by permission, I've used actual names of the individuals...

For the sake of simplicity, the author has chosen to use the masculine pronoun "him" when referring to an unnamed individual.

CONTENTS:

Freedom exists not so you can do what you like. It exists so you can do what you ought!

-Jim Caviezel

Acknowledgments

I'm not sure anyone ever reads the acknowledgment section of a book unless they know they are being acknowledged.

But you should.

You just may get a bit of inspiration—whether it be a point made or a name mentioned—that will be the catalyst for your success.

In my youth I truly believed people were self-made. After all, it seemed most of my idols professed that their success in business, in life and in wealth was all because of their efforts—and their efforts alone. They acknowledged no one but themselves.

Perhaps they really didn't have anyone to acknowledge and maybe their success truly was because of their efforts alone.

But that doesn't apply to me.

I am the sum of those whom I have allowed to speak into my life and those who have partnered with me on some great projects—and even on some not-so-great projects.

I've learned just as much from my failures, if not more, than I have from my successes. Here's a quick tip: Don't be afraid to fail…but don't let your failures define you. If you are surrounded by the right people, you'll have a number of folks to acknowledge because they will help you through both the good times and the "is it over yet" times.

First and foremost, I thank my wife. She is the definition of resilient. Yes, I know. It seems this word is over-used, but in her case, it truly applies. She empowers me and fills the gaps when I'm traveling, working long hours, or locked in the basement writing. And, she does it with a smile. You'll want to ask her to share some stories should you ever meet her because she definitely has them.

Not everyone thanks their in-laws, but I have reason to. They have always treated me as their favorite son-in-law (most likely because I'm their only son-in-law) and have always been supportive despite my flaws and despite my taking their daughter on some pretty wild business ventures.

I loved the comradery of the military and I was fortunate enough to be able to build those types of relationships in my civilian life. I have several men in my life who make up my "band of brothers" and speak truth. See, truth will set you free—you can either surround yourself with "yes" men, or men and women who will speak boldly and truthfully into your life. I finally allowed the latter after falling on my face a few times. Bea, Hogan, Vatter, Canfield, and Leonard—thank you.

P & A Thomas, thanks for giving me a hand-up when I needed it most.

There have been several who always have stood alongside this mission to help bring transformation and attention to our veteran issues: Reeves, Grant, Waddingham, J & B Kenney, thank you for your steadfast commitment. J & B, your support has been both humbling and a Godsend.

I also thank those who volunteered to be interviewed. The stories shared here are personal— and the names aren't fictitious. I labored over the details of these stories, not to make me look good, but rather to bring honor to the lives of those who chose to be vulnerable so others can benefit. I'm grateful.

I'm also grateful to those who chose to endorse this book. Any time someone puts his support behind someone else's work, there is risk. Association is powerful in both a positive and negative way. These endorsements are a great reminder to me to always be humble and to be a source of inspiration.

Finally, on the acknowledgments at least, I'd be nothing without my faith. Don't panic, I'm not going to preach here. What I will say is that because of my faith in God, I've learned to trust more. There is freedom in trusting those in your life and trusting something greater than one's self. God has been a comforting constant for me, even when I've lacked faith. What is your constant and where do you put your faith? I'm just asking.

I'm not self-made. I really am the sum of those who are in my life and what I choose to apply to my life. Self-made is for the narcissist. I'm far from that. And while not self-made, I am certainly motivated, dedicated and persistent—and I take action. That does require self.

In your life, at the very least, strive to be: motivated, dedicated, persistent, faithful and action oriented. You'll be in for a journey when you are.

Lastly, acknowledge those in your life who are helping shape the person you are today.

Author's Note

I'll admit it—I cried. The video was that powerful. Two dear friends and I were sitting around the office conference room table reaching for tissue after witnessing a mom, who recently returned from a deployment, surprise her school-aged son at a basketball game. The son, who had no clue of mom's return, had just missed his second free throw, but upon the miss, mom walked out on the court and whispered, "It's okay, baby. Your mom will always love you." At the sound of his mom's voice, the young man dropped to his knees, without even looking at his mom, and cried. His mom walked over, knelt down beside him and just wrapped him up in her arms. The high school audience went crazy in celebration.

And three grown men were left crying in a conference room.

It hit me at that moment that the hug and the celebration are just the beginning. There is a lot of life that happens after the hug. For the mom and son, there was no doubt a lot of catching up to do. For just the mom, months of getting reacquainted with how her talents and skills could best be applied in her civilian life.

Our service members' life stories don't stop after the tearful homecoming. Typically, they only make the headlines again because of poverty, unemployment, suicide or divorce.

The media-generated conversation and perception often surrounding veterans and their families in America is completely wrong. All warriors aren't wounded and all veterans aren't broken—but America seems to focus only on these struggles.

It's time for Americans to pay closer attention to what really happens after the airport homecoming.

What happens once a service member returns—when teamed with the right plan and a strong support network—is fundamentally changing America.

Less than 7 percent of the U.S. population has served the U.S. in uniform. The 7 percent—the percentage of U.S. citizens who are veterans—learned how to work efficiently and effectively under pressure, can manage crisis, are able to win hearts and minds and adapt quickly—all while focusing on mission success. And they continue to exercise what they learned after their homecoming hugs.

Here's what I hope you learn from this book: first and foremost that not all veterans are broken or wounded. Even those who have PTSD, which are a small percentage, should not be cast aside. All veterans have more to contribute after service. Their mission to serve America is not over when they take off the uniform.

When you finish this book, don't just put it on the shelf and let it collect dust. Share it with industry leaders and educators. Knowledge and insight are effective change agents when they are shared.

Finally, if you are in education or are responsible for hiring talent, pay close attention to that veteran who walks in your door. He or she may not have the skills, but guaranteed they have the character and aptitude you are looking for. This person is truly America's greatest asset.

Preface

Jack stepped off the plane and scanned the hundred or so families that were anxiously waiting the return of their warfighter. The mission had not been easy. In fact, it had been filled with many silent prayers and close calls, the kind that always failed to make the headlines. Now he was home, and like the families on the other side of the fence that separated the waiting area from the tarmac, Jack couldn't wait to hug his wife of 10 years and their two young daughters. And while he knew that this was his last deployment, Jack knew his mission was far from over.

We've all watched dozens of videos or read countless articles celebrating the warfighter's return home. Jack's homecoming hug and the viral videos of Jack—or Bob or John or Mike—surprising their loved ones with an unexpected return home are common. The race to embrace after the return from some battle-torn wasteland has caused many tears, has rallied much political support, and has driven people to buy "support our troops" bumper stickers or tie yellow ribbons around their antennas and bridge overpasses.

And while America sheds a thankful and grateful tear as it watches Jack embrace, many fail to grasp what makes Jack the best hope for America: his never-quit, do-whatever-it-takes attitude to overcome not just one major life struggle, but often, years of struggle. Until victory is achieved.

The celebratory homecoming hug that makes America cry is just the start to America's real solution and one of Jack's most difficult missions and struggles:

> The mission to not only find his or her purpose after service but the struggle to adapt, change, and ultimately overcome America's perception in order to help solve America's problems.

American industry is slowly catching on. The effort to hire veterans in this country has improved tremendously over the past five years. The 100,000 Jobs Mission pioneered by JPMorgan Chase & Co in 2011 with only 11 companies has grown to more than 190 companies hiring more than 200,000 veterans.

According to a 2015 nationwide survey by Harris Poll, on behalf of CareerBuilder, of the more than 2,500 responses from hiring and human resources managers, nearly half (47 percent) said "they pay more attention to the applications submitted by veterans, and 69 percent said that if given two equally qualified candidates—one veteran and one not—they are more likely to hire the veteran." (source: (Maurer, 2015))

This is a significant improvement from 2010 when nearly half suggested they were "less favorable" to hiring veterans.

But there is still much work to do—not only in industry, but in our colleges and universities, in whom we elect, and certainly in the American mindset.

Since my previous book, *Operation Military Family: How Military Couples are Fighting to Preserve their Marriages*, I've spent the past eight years helping military and veteran families transition from a wartime mentality to a peacetime mission; and, I have seen them struggle—with poverty, unemployment, suicidal thoughts, homelessness, or understanding the new normal in their personal and professional relationships. It is this journey to overcome the struggle, the fight to overcome the battles at home, both the personal and professional, that is forging a battle-hardened, yet street smart and skilled talent pool that ultimately will help restore America to that "shining city on a hill."[ii]

While industry is starting to catch on to this rich talent pool, many Americans still think today's warfighter is broken, or suffering from Post-Traumatic Stress, or is severely wounded.

America as a whole has yet to embrace today's veteran warfighter as a viable solution to our workforce needs. Americans, historically, have focused on the veterans' problems or their struggles. Instead, though, we need to realize that because of the veterans' experience serving *mission above self,* then overcoming the roadblocks faced once they arrive home, today's veteran is America's true hope for positive change.

What follows are several stories highlighting only a few of the veterans who not only have served their country with honors but also are considered by most people to be a success.

But let me first define what I mean by success, because in today's environment we throw that word around to define anything that doesn't outright fail. Even the most average of accomplishments is often labeled a "success." After all, everyone gets a trophy just for participating.

These individuals you'll meet faced tremendous challenges—some in theatre, some on the home front and some in both arenas. But they didn't let their challenges or struggles define them or stop them. They are far from the average "Joe" who gives up or riots because he is unemployed, has debt, isn't part of the upper class, has financial difficulty, or is discriminated against.

To succeed, they got back up. They decided their circumstances would not define them. And, while they didn't expect government handouts like many of today's Americans, they did expect the government to honor its promise for veteran benefits without delay.

They are the veterans who have become impact players in their communities and in their industries. One individual built up a successful attorney/client phone consultation business, another helped automate and change how industry does payroll, one couple helps other military and veteran couples improve their relationships, another is making an impact in technology with a major defense-sector contractor, while yet another is helping change how a state cares and positions its returning veterans. This is what I mean by success: veterans who stand out. They have risen above their issues and have silenced the murmurs that they, like all the rest of their brothers and sisters who have served, are broken, or unemployable, or suffering from PTSD, or are some walking time bomb waiting to detonate.

These are America's problem solvers—true warriors who worked to overcome their own struggles, established a plan, then leaned in to a support network in order to help change America. And, what changes they have made!

Chapter 1
GRIT – What America Needs

Grit. Perhaps what America needs is less polish and more grit. Not the riot type grit—real grit. Our high school grads enter the safe environment of our colleges and universities to become book smart, checklist-perfect recruits for today's work place. Some have long-practiced skills to help them nail the interviews. They might even have ample "volunteer service" at the soup kitchen or old folks' home.

But what about grit? What about that character-defining experience, or that sixth sense, or that honed skill and know-how that is so critical to an ever-changing, dynamic economy where one day everything is good to go and the next America is rocked to the core by a stock market drop, terrorist attack, or natural disaster? The type of grit that can only be earned.

Deployments aren't easy. They are tough on families. Some survive, some don't. But through them, grit is developed. Grit is a trait that can't be taught—it can only be earned. The change in mission requirements, the uncertainty of outcomes, the disconnect from the home front, the need to think and react quickly while being patient and methodical, the ability to work with people you don't like but need to cooperate with in order to accomplish the mission.

Deployments likewise refine and hone the character and aptitude of each person associated with them. They require the individual to dig deep and discover who they really are and what they are made of. Not everyone survives this intense heat. It's like forging steel. The individual is not perfect—most likely he or she is rough around the edges and has soft skills that need a bit of polishing. But character? Aptitude? Both are rock-solid.

This is grit.

* * *

Frank was ready. This deployment—his second—was intended to help the Anbar province establish a functional government. No easy task. Courts were closed, Iraqis were being jailed and held without any hope of due process, and his "Rule of Law" team was organized to "fix it."

Frank had plans to "fix" his personal life as well.

As he prepped, he reflected on how much had changed since his first deployment. It was on his first deployment in Iraq that he was notified that he had passed the bar exam. Frank had completed his undergraduate degree and then enrolled in both law school and the National Guard while in his thirties. He hoped these moves would help pull him from the depression brought on by a failed marriage. His wife of five years and mother of his three children, walked out on him during the summer before his senior year of ministerial school. Being a lawyer was quite different than being a minister.

This deployment would also be quite different from his first. Frank paused for a moment and recalled how on his first deployment he was strongly in favor of bringing democracy to Iraq and was prepared to defend with his life the mission to bring freedom to an oppressed people.

But after serving as the intel non-commissioned officer (NCO) to a special, independent 30-person company, the 116th RAOC, Frank came to believe his government had lied and that this war was more about protecting American special interests than transplanting freedom.

All that was going to change on this second deployment. The deception of "no boots on the ground" and the haunting cover-ups would all be solved. Even the "wedding" incident, this plausible deniability incident—if, in fact, true—well, that, Frank determined, likewise would be resolved. He recalled:

Intelligence intercepted cell calls about a "wedding," a code word for a gathering of Islamic terrorist cell leaders with someone from higher up in their organization. Frank communicated on a scrambled SAT phone the arrival of the first "guests" to the location. About 20 males were busy with preparations including a lone male who never seemed to remove his eyes from the road from the south. A few men disappeared into the only house in the area. This location previously had been unknown as a cell location, which strengthened the indication of a high level meeting. Knowing planes en-route carried precision missiles, his job now was to set a laser beam for their guidance systems to follow to this exact location. Fifteen minutes later a few of the men start gesturing. Three vehicles approach, all black Mercedes. He calls in the hit; "target arriving." On this mission the target was not anyone in particular. Back in the U.S., the President's low approval numbers meant yet another mission directed from the Pentagon by people who knew little of the local situation. Directives "from the highest level" set up a mission where we would strike first and sort out the bodies later. If we killed a high-level target, so much the better, but that was not as important as a successful air strike announced by the President on international television. This soldier hated politics, and was glad to be as far away from D.C. as possible. His final two steps: alert local authorities about the completion of the air strike and successfully disengage before they arrived. He focused his long-range binoculars on a man smiling as he reached for the back door of the third Mercedes. The door opened. A gloved hand reached out, a white dress emerged. The bride's smile turned to horror as the missile hits precisely on target and on time. Over 30 innocent locals dead. Intel got it wrong. This was a real wedding.

Frank landed and the first thing he noticed was the intense heat. The Anbar province is the largest province in Iraq and shares its borders with Syria, Jordan, and Saudi Arabia. It feels more like it shares a border with the sun. His "Rule of Law" team would be responsible for working with the tribal leaders and the U.S. hand-picked local government to establish some sort of order to a region that was similar to the Wild West.

Frank entered the building and shook his head. State of the art equipment, computers, and files sat in piles covered with layers of sand storm dust. Millions of dollars of U.S. taxpayer money just going to waste. The tribal leaders still worked out accidents between tribes like they had in centuries past, not like it should be in 2009. They'd meet, agree to an equitable resolution and the guilty parties would agree to the consequence or to the restitution the tribal leaders worked out. In a split second Frank knew that he was tasked with getting the locals to adopt a system they didn't want.

In 2004 Frank came to realize on his first deployment that if the U.S. had a true volunteer army, people who disagreed with the premise of the mission or war would be allowed to opt-out. After all, in most careers, if you decide you want to leave your job because there is a values-disconnect, you can. You give notice and walk. Not so in the military.

When you sign your name and raise your right hand you are committing your life, in some cases literally, to the service of this country, regardless of the intent and purpose of the mission. It is a selfless act—one that only 7 percent of the population living in America makes. Mission above self. At that very moment, you are suddenly at the whim of the political machine. For many, this is a wake-up call from the free will, everyone's-opinion-has-value, do-what-you-want-when-you-want, relatively safe childhood most of today's American youth experience.

His first deployment was a goat rope in so many ways. But Frank knew his second tour would be a vast improvement. He lost part of his soul on that first deployment and now questioned the motives that were coming from the government. The war had changed everything. The world was less safe and, in his mind, people less trustworthy.

It was also on the first deployment that Frank received an e-mail from his son asking if he was okay. Of course, he was, but his son needed him to find some way—any way—to call him. His son had just received a phone call from someone posing as a military member telling him that his dad had been killed in action. His son was an emotional wreck, was angry with God, and couldn't get a grip until he could actually hear Frank's voice. That experience was seared in Frank's mind.

When Frank had returned from his first deployment, he attempted to put the war behind him and start over. But that was far from easy. His blast injury from an enemy-improvised explosive device had rendered him without the use of his legs for months, hooked on pills and sentenced to months of therapy to learn how to walk again. Despite the injury, he wrote a book and focused on trying to be a good dad to his kids and a good husband to his second wife.

As Frank sifted through the heaps of taxpayer waste, he was convinced this second deployment would be the ultimate game changer.

Several months into his deployment, Frank sat in his military-assigned trailer—his home away from home—with nothing to do but sort through memories. Iraq was a hellhole the first time...and the second time. The Iraqis wanted nothing to do with this "modern" style of governing. Frank sat back and reflected on how his book failed to gain any traction between deployments, how his second marriage was now strained, and his spiritual life—which at one point was the most important part of his life—was in a dark place.

Frank had convinced himself that he had no reason to live.

Grit. Every painful moment, every failed relationship, the disappointments, the unmet expectations...some let these circumstances define them, others think death is the ultimate problem solver, and still others find a way to dig deep and rise up. But this takes grit and sometimes grit is hard to find:

> I felt at peace with my decision. A voice beckoned, "this way and all will be well." Death, the ultimate problem solver.

Frank waited for the range to clear from the night fire qualifications and for the majority of troops to head to the dining facility before he went to the upper room. He loaded a magazine into the well and chambered a round.

As Frank cradled the weapon, sweat dripping down his face from the heat, flashbacks of his 2004 conversation with his son receiving the false news of him being killed in action overtook him. He could see his son curled up in agony. He could hear his cries and feel his pain.

The M-16 shook in Frank's hands as he wrestled mentally with conflicting thoughts to end it all or to embrace the suck and press on. Frank moved the selector switch from safe to semi. His hand wouldn't stop shaking. If he missed, the damages could be irreparable and he'd still be alive. He couldn't miss. But he couldn't shake the vision of his son screaming at the news of his death.

After several minutes of shaking, Frank laid down the weapon.

This is the grit no one wants to talk about. But it was this experience—this life changing moment—that actually put Frank on his path to success.

It's true that Frank found himself deep in a place that most people don't want to talk about. He felt like a failure as a father, wanted a better life for his kids, was unhappy with some of the decisions he had made and didn't know how to deal with his physical, emotional, and spiritual pain.

The growing phone consultation business he had built up after his first deployment was all but dead. And his second marriage was ending in divorce. Everything he had focused his skills and abilities on was a mess.

He wanted to give up. It would have been easy. But if there was one thing that Frank came to realize through his experiences on his tours was that dying because he was unhappy wasn't reason enough. Men and women just like him were dying almost every day, but they had died with and for a purpose. He wanted to be a man *on purpose.*

We all read the journals touting the successful businessman or woman and covet their success—but would we want their success if we knew their struggle? Maybe not. But I'm guessing we'd want to hire that individual.

While not everyone who deploys deals with suicidal thoughts or intentions, most deal with the emotional, mental, and physical uncertainty that comes with every deployment. They develop a certain amount of scar tissue and resiliency that today's inexperienced college graduate has yet to experience.

Our veterans know what *mission above self* means. They learn to long for purpose, not just a paycheck.

That twenty-something kid fresh from a deployment who may or may not have a degree has likely managed more individuals, dealt with more chaos, and had to adapt more quickly to a change in mission than most individuals in their thirties—maybe even many people in their forties. And while he or she is likely rough around the edges when it comes to interview skills, that same individual has likely interfaced with a wide range of demographics and cultures.

They are ready. That deployment has prepared them for almost anything corporate America or small business can throw at them.

They have a highly refined ability to compartmentalize situations that even some of the most seasoned executives lack. Their deployments have assured they have gained wisdom beyond their years.

Frank is now happily remarried and lives with purpose. He'll tell you he's glad that he didn't succeed at suicide and is thrilled that he is succeeding in his family and his business. In his words, "Today I am a positive presence in my children's lives. I am happily remarried, my career is better than ever. I have more joy, peace, comfort, and love in my life than I ever thought possible."

Frank occasionally volunteers to help people who are struggling with the thought of suicide. He's plugged in to the VA—despite all the horror stories—and has also found a new spiritual home.

He's writing a second book, *The Suicide Solution* that will help people understand why suicide looks attractive but isn't the answer. In it he explains what some of the tools are and how to use them to prevent a growing problem.

Frank's success is gritty. It's not the fairy tale story we like to read about or watch. But we must. Because Frank, and people like him, are making a local impact. He is saving lives and changing conversations.

The skills Frank leverages from his deployments and his struggles are what make him incredibly easy to talk to and relate to today. These same skills—listening, adapting quickly, measuring all options, enduring difficult situations, navigating emotional turmoil, and more—are the very same skills today's transitioning service members have developed.

Perhaps, this is the type of grit—this overcoming after exploring every option—is what America needs first to recognize and then to embrace.

CHAPTER 2
ADAPTABILITY – Being Flexible When it Counts

The adapt and overcome adage isn't just for the strong-minded or some CrossFit gym poster. The ability to adjust and adapt to new conditions quickly and smoothly is required of almost every productive person in America—especially if he plans to do more than "just survive."

But change isn't easy. Most prefer routines. Most operate under "this is how it's done" or "I'm stuck in my ways," and even cringe at the thought of having to retrain in order to retain employment, even though this often is mandated by their company. So individuals pack their bags seeking employment with a company that will hire them to do what "they've always done." Their skills rise to the top, but character and adaptability fall to second tier.

For the general public, change is difficult.

Not the case for veterans. America's veterans have been trained to adapt to ensure their mission, whatever it is, succeeds. Change is part of who they are. No longer are there maps hanging on walls highlighting fixed locations of enemy combatants—those all have been replaced by whiteboards and erasers to capture the fluidity of the mission. Those wearing the uniform are expected to carry out the mission as described, but have been trained to expect the mission to change. That training follows them into civilian life.

Adapt and overcome—because this is how you survive.

* * *

"Frankly, Steve, you aren't worth my time." The recruiter, who was prior military, looked at Steve with some compassion and spoke directly—which Steve appreciated. The recruiter continued, "I am graded on how fast I fill my open positions. I get what you had to go through to become a Navy Captain. But, I can sell them a less capable candidate they can understand faster than I can sell them you Steve, so you are not worth my time."

It was beginning to make sense. His 25-year career as a sailor in the world's greatest Navy meant little to the 20-something Millennials who were now recruiting and managing today's talent. It's not that they didn't care, they simply didn't understand Steve's experience. He wasn't a "check the box" candidate. While senior-level management was looking for competency and organizational value, the mid-20-something recruiters were looking for hard skills—skills that didn't seem to match Steve's.

Steve nodded, thanked the recruiter for his honesty and input, and promptly exited the building.

I'll figure it out, thought Steve. How life had changed since his Southern California days.

Steve grew up in a culture of service under the bright sun of Southern California. His dad was a combat-injured WWII veteran and service to country was always at the top of the list and called to him.

It was a pathway he desired.

Shortly after high school, Steve was hired as a 911 operator and police/fire dispatcher by the City of Milpitas. This position served as a stepping-stone to the Reserve Police Academy where he became a Reserve Police Officer for the city before leaving to finish his bachelor's degree at U.C. Santa Barbara.

Life was good. Even before his mid-twenties, he had some practical life experience serving his community—beyond the typical volunteer work most high school grads accomplish before college—and college was proving to be a blast.

Then the movie Top Gun hit the big screen. The year was 1986. The bright white uniforms, the comradery, the thrill—Steve knew this was his next mission, all except the Top Gun part. With his eyesight there was no way the Navy was letting him near the business end of a jet. With his bachelor's degree in hand, he met with an Officer Recruiter and prepared his application package for consideration. Like most programs in the military, the selection process is competitive.

Fortunately, Steve was selected and off he went to Officer Candidate School in Newport, Rhode Island.

OCS, as Officer Candidate School is typically referred as, is an intense 16-week course designed to give the recruit a working knowledge of the Navy, both afloat and ashore. It can be a shock to someone who has been pampered and coddled through their upbringing or in their education. It prepares every individual who can muster the mental and physical strength to assume the responsibilities of a Naval Officer—one of the most respected positions in the military.

OCS is extremely demanding; morally, mentally, and physically. Honor, Courage, and Commitment aren't just slogans—these are core values that will be challenged and tested. Academically one has to excel or he'll wash out. Attention to detail at every level will be inspected and expected. And while one's mind is being sharpened, their body will be pushed to extreme physical limits. Not everyone makes it. But Steve was dedicated and committed.

This is what is required of every Naval Officer. And Steve graduated.

The Navy, like all the other branches, allows one to select where they want to serve and then often sends the individual to some location they never considered. Steve asked for a ship on the West Coast—after all, California was familiar territory—so, naturally, he was sent to Norfolk, Virginia.

Steve reported for duty to the USS NASSAU (LHA-4), a Tarawa-class amphibious assault ship. This was to be the start of many opportunities to adapt and change if he was to advance in his career.

Commissioned at Pascagoula, Mississippi on July 28, 1979, the USS NASSAU integrated some of the Navy's most complex weapons systems, automated cargo handling, and state-of-the-art propulsion into a huge hull, forming a ship with a wide range of mission capabilities. Those capabilities included amphibious warfare, anti-surface warfare, anti-air warfare, and power projection ashore, utilizing helicopters and Very Short Take-Off and Landing (VSTOL) Aircraft.

The NASSAU was capable of transporting more than 3,000 United States Navy and United States Marine Corps personnel. She was impressive.

Steve started as 1st Division Officer of the ship's deck department, the spot where most junior sailors without a rating—otherwise known as a vocation—start. He and his young sailors were not only responsible for safely receiving, discharging, and caring for cargo during a voyage, they also were responsible for the maintenance and upkeep of the ship. There was always paint to chip and a surface to paint.

It wasn't long before the NASSAU was "haze gray and underway"—a tribal term used by surface ship crews to distinguish themselves from submarine crews. Steve found himself vomiting over the side as his new home navigated the high seas of the North Atlantic...and wondering why he had thought the Navy would be a good idea.

The NASSAU was getting its fair share of high profile press. And Steve was quickly learning that in order to succeed and advance, one must quickly learn to adapt.

In August of 1988, NASSAU departed for Teamwork 88, acting as flagship for Commander, Amphibious Strike Force/Commander, Amphibious Group Two and Commander, Marine Striking Force Atlantic/4th Marine Expeditionary Brigade. Teamwork 88 was the largest multi-national exercise of the 1980s in defense of Norway to thwart a possible Soviet Maritime threat against allied sea-lanes. The exercise was designed to force U.S. commanders to reconsider tactics in the conduct of Harpoon missile strikers, mine-laying missions, and air-to-air combat. It also allowed NATO to evaluate its ability to conduct a maritime campaign in the Norwegian Sea and project forces ashore in northern Norway.

Teamwork 88 was a huge success. As a result of the team's continued frontline activities and successful missions throughout 1988 and 1989, the USS NASSAU was selected by the Commander, Naval Surface Force,

Atlantic as the top LHA for the Battle Efficiency competitive cycle, earning the ship her second Battle "E" in her 10 years of commissioned service. Steve was honored to be a part of that crew's success.

Steve continued to find himself on numerous successful missions—whether it was delivering 81,000 lbs. of relief supplies for victims of Hurricane Gilbert or rescuing 172 Haitian nationals from an unseaworthy craft. He also had moved from deck department to engineering as the MP1 (the Main Propulsion 1st Officer), though he had little background in or knowledge about engineering. He had to learn the required hard skills quickly if he was to maintain mission and ship success.

In early February, Steve and the rest of the NASSAU crew found themselves conducting operations in the Caribbean; operations which ultimately resulted in supporting a drug summit between President George H.W. Bush and the leaders of three South American countries that were meeting to discuss the worldwide peril of international drug trafficking. More accolades followed.

Steve continued to be an impact team member. He proved he could learn quickly and provide solid leadership even when he had uncertainty. Steve never allowed his lack of knowledge to hold him back—he would just research, adapt, and figure it out.

The USS NASSAU crew was used to adapting. With only eight days' notice, Steve and the crew deployed for eight-and-a-half months to the Middle East. After mobilizing and onloading the 4th Marine Expeditionary Battalion in record time, the sailors left the United States as the flagship for the Commander of the Amphibious Task Force and the 4th MEB's Commanding General. On Feb. 21, 1991, Marine AV-8Bs conducted bombing runs off the flight deck of USS Nassau. The crew made history.

During this extended combat deployment Steve was one of three officers who routinely served as Officer of the Deck when NASSAU was underway. The round-the-clock rotation of four hours on and eight hours off was in addition to his regular assignment in the Engineering Department. Steve was an example of the NASSAU crews' commitment to excellence and her ability to adapt based on mission requirements.

This event was the first time ever that Marine AV-8B jump jets conducted combat missions from a helicopter assault ship.

During Steve's three-year tour on the USS NASSAU, he racked up a number of mission successes, not because of his efforts alone, but because of his team's resolve to accomplish every mission with excellence. Steve walked in to his first assignment a naïve sailor, but learned to adapt quickly to new assignments and situations depending on what was required in the moment.

Steve's first Surface Warfare Officer Department Head assignment took him to the West Coast, where he reported for duty as the Engineering Officer for the steam-powered USS Fort Fisher, an Anchorage-class dock landing ship. While Steve had attended department head school, a six-month shore-based intense course on leadership, he was assigned a department he knew little about: propulsion and auxiliaries.

Steve was not a mechanical genius. Having been a main propulsion division officer and Engineering Officer of the Watch (EOOW) qualified at his previous ship, it only made sense that he would now be in charge of the Fort Fisher's steam turbines. Steve accepted the challenge; his option was to either give up or learn as fast as he could—and he was quickly learning how to be a subject-matter expert when he didn't even really know the subject.

As Steve progressed in his career, he continued to seek opportunities and take assignments that would push him outside his comfort zone. He knew that whatever the assignment, there was a strong chance he could figure it out and learn the skill.

This commitment to continued learning and adapting earned him a selection to the U.S. Naval War College in Newport, Rhode Island. Prior to this selection, Steve had taken assignments in Tennessee to be the Human Resource Officer. From deck department, engineering, operations, to human resources, Steve was quick on his feet to learn the skills required of the assignment.

He was becoming a master of adapting and overcoming.

The War College once again pushed Steve to new limits. Here he honed both his strategic and tactical abilities, and expanded his know-how on what is required to strengthen maritime security and combat readiness. He was introduced to leaders across the country who would challenge him on what he thought was the "right approach" to a situation, and he truly embraced the charge of the college's thirty-seventh president, Vice Admiral Stansfield Turner, who challenged not only the college, but the leaders she was training to "always keep in mind...the country's need of military leaders with the capability of solving complex problems and executing their decisions. You must keep your sights set on decision making or problem solving as your objective."

Steve agreed. What America needed most were leaders who could not only make decisions, but execute on their decisions. Specific hard skills mattered, but not nearly as much as leadership.

Steve soon found himself assigned to work for the Vice Chief of Naval Operations, the second highest-ranking commissioned officer in the United States Navy. Steve was part of the team that assisted the VCNO in making institutional improvements throughout the Navy. No small task, but his journey had prepared him well. No matter the task or skill required—adapt and overcome.

He continued to rack up the experience, the achievement medals, the letters of commendation, as well as command of a ship. It certainly wasn't without challenges—his decision to stay the course with the Navy cost him his first marriage. He threw himself into his work, embracing the demands of the job and the fast pace. Eventually, he found true love, remarried and was blessed not only with a great family, but also orders to the Pacific Northwest.

The orders to the Pacific Northwest couldn't have come at a better time. Close to nearing the end of his career, Steve and his wife decided the Seattle area would be a great place to retire from the Navy and start again—after all, Seattle was rich with opportunities in high tech and was known to be military friendly.

Steve got to the Navy Reserve Center in Bremerton where he took command and was charged with the success of 1000 Naval Reservists through the Navy Reserve's Full Time Support (FTS) program. FTS was a program in which active duty sailors were tasked with supporting those who were in the Navy reserve.

This turned out to be a great assignment for Steve, as this was his final two-year tour and with the Navy being an "advance up or out" organization where only so many people can move up, Steve, with his limited time, was not slotted to advance. Instead of seeing this as a shortcoming, Steve viewed it as an opportunity—much like he did every past assignment. The Bremerton Reserve Center provided Steve the opportunity to better understand the civilian landscape through the eyes of his reservists.

With his own transition to the civilian sector quickly approaching, Steve would ask his reservists about their civilian careers, including what they liked, what skills were beneficial and what they leveraged from their military experience in their civilian jobs. He wanted to know what made these reservists, at least those who were employed, successful.

But many of his reservists weren't employed. And those who struggled to find civilian work were also struggling with their reservist duties.

Steve was facing a challenge he hadn't faced ever before while on active duty: how to help a reservist find a job after serving a 12-month active duty mobilization tour. Many who had civilian jobs prior to their deployments returned home to find they no longer had employment.

Being a reservist had unforeseen consequences for many of his young sailors.

Steve set out to help solve this issue for his sailors. To serve and then to face unemployment after serving was an unacceptable outcome for Steve or his reservists to accept. He had experienced many mission successes and was determined to see this one succeed as well.

As he began to explore possible options in the market place, Steve came across Hire America's Heroes, a local Seattle-based organization founded by Major General James Collins, U.S. Army, retired.

Major General Collins, who expected people to call him "Jimmy," was not only the founder of Hire America's Heroes, but also the state's Civilian Aide to the Secretary of the Army, and he had the ear of almost every major CEO in the Seattle region.

The mission of Hire America's Heroes was to connect America's major corporations, especially those in the Seattle area, with the rich skills and abilities of military service members and their families for the purpose of employment in the corporate workforce.

Steve had a mission to accomplish himself, so he made a point to meet Jimmy. Steve had the talent, Hire America's Heroes had the corporations. Reservists needed jobs and corporations needed the talent. This appeared to be a perfect marriage. And as he explored the situation further, the relationship turned out to be fruitful.

The organization not only provided mentorship to some of his young sailors, but also to Steve as he neared his own transition date. He once again wanted to stretch his abilities and learn what value he could bring to the civilian sector beyond just driving ships or being in the merchant marines.

As weeks turned into months, the Admiral of Navy Region Northwest asked Steve to be the formal liaison to the civilian sector. His informal relationship with Hire America's Heroes was now being sanctioned as official. This not only cleared some red tape, it also accelerated the exposure his reservists were getting to corporations through on-base job fairs.

Steve also was helping senior management in the civilian sector understand the military, many of whom knew little beyond what they were exposed to through the media or movies. He was overcoming myths and answering their questions, while they were shedding light on what they viewed as key issues, like the ability to relate or get along, or move beyond tasks and to be flexible on assignments. Perception, however it was acquired, often had many of the executives thinking the young man or woman in uniform would be rigid and unrelenting in the work place, and Steve was there to help correct that myth. After all, his many years of service had taught him that being able to adapt—and sometimes quickly—was a requirement to success.

Steve was accomplishing three missions at once: helping his reservists, helping senior management in the civilian sector, and helping better prepare himself for civilian life.

His transition to the civilian sector was sure to be a successful one. Most likely his most successful mission.

In the spring of 2011, 18 months before he was to transition, Steve started to compile his resumé. Could such a simple task be so difficult? Steve struggled. He had a hard time pulling in the hard budget numbers he was in charge of simply because he never had to pay attention to the size of his budgets. Operational cycles kept the numbers ever changing. His budgets, whether they were hundreds of thousands, millions or hundreds of millions, operated under the premise of "the number isn't important—your job is to just do the most you can with what you got." The number didn't matter. The mission mattered, and that trumped any budget number.

How does one communicate on a resumé a moving target budget that is influenced by operational cycles and politics?

Steve also struggled with the coaching he was receiving to highlight his accomplishments and successes. This was a major shift in his cultural mindset. Every success he had over his 20 plus years was always a "we" thing, not an "I" thing. Yet, the resumé was all about "I."

Regardless of the resumé, because of Steve's rank as a Navy Captain— one of the most respected ranks in the Navy—he was continually being told that corporate needed smart, capable leaders like him. Senior and executive leaders assured him he was the "executive level infielder" they needed.

So his resumé remained a bit vague and locked in military speak because it was obvious he wouldn't need his resumé.

Despite the assurances, Steve continued to do a lot of informational interviews so he could better understand how his military experience was relevant and valuable to the civilian sector. This knowledge also allowed him to provide better coaching to his young reservists. He had two goals while still serving as command: help his reservists exceed their performance goals while on duty and help his reservists gain employment. The two influenced each other greatly.

As he got closer to transition, Steve focused his efforts on applying to the large companies—after all, this is where he had the most connections and they are very public about their desires and goals to hire veterans. But what senior management failed to communicate to Steve, or failed to understand themselves...or what Steve failed to pick up on, was that the large companies required every applicant to go through a process and the process didn't recognize the military skill set or competencies. The process wants a "check the box" candidate—someone they can "plug and play."

Steve found he was dealing with a different level of individual in the hiring process—the senior management would pass Steve to the hiring team, generally someone in her mid-20s who was focused on the hard skills.

The time finally came for Steve, his family, and many of his young sailors, to celebrate his retirement. Twenty-five years of true service to the United States Navy. He had traveled the world, he had participated in many great missions, oversaw big and small budgets, trained on some of the top equipment in the world, commanded thousands, was mentored by the best and was a personal mentor to hundreds over his many years of service.

But now, Steve was being told he didn't have the right hard-skills.

Steve got in his car, took a breath, looked in the rear-view mirror, and thought, *Now what?*

Frustrated and more than a bit disillusioned, Steve began to wonder if all his years of training, his years of command, his commitment to excellence, his top-level clearances, and his dedicated laser focus on making connections at the highest corporate levels prior to transition, would pay off. While he had no regrets regarding his Navy career—none—this last interview, if that's what you could call it, made it quite clear that hiring managers needed a specific person with specific skills.

He started the car, put it in drive, and began to head back to base housing.

This was a high stress time. He was now retired, but still living in base housing. Command had given him an extension, but he had to vacate soon—real soon.

For the first time in his life, he had no idea where he was going to work or where to move his family. This was the first "transfer" where he had no idea what was going to happen.

The perception of those around him, both in the Navy and outside the Navy, was that since he was a senior officer, he most certainly had jobs lined up. The reality was Steve was facing an experience bias. He didn't fit the executive management mold for a lot of hiring managers and he couldn't get the lower-end jobs because hiring managers were certain he quickly would move onto something better.

His life in the Navy was all about completing an assignment regardless of whether he liked it—and he did so 100 percent of the time. He made it work; he added value regardless of the assignment and environment.

Now, he couldn't even get a chance to add value. He began to understand personally what many of his reservists faced after their short 12-month deployment and being disconnected from the civilian world. Imagine being "disconnected" for 25 years.

Industry spoke a good game, but they struggled to let the players they publicly professed they wanted on the field to play positions that had meaning. It wasn't corporate leadership that was telling Steve he couldn't be a great "position player"—it was the hiring managers. In their eyes Steve was at best qualified to be the water boy.

But giving up wasn't an option.

Steve was invited to a military outreach event by a large company. A who's who session that sounded promising. Senior management talked about where the company was going, the victories they expected to have and the challenges they faced. Their "gap analysis" clearly stated how they needed military leaders with Steve's type of experience. From his own assessment, this seemed to be the answer.

The next part of the event was a mixer with hiring managers where hopeful candidates or job seekers were given the opportunity to mingle and talk with those who actually did the hiring. Steve shared what he had learned from the senior management session, his enthusiasm for solving problems and adding value. The hiring managers smiled, nodded their heads, and then confirmed what the military recruiter had shared with

Steve weeks earlier—they didn't care about the gaps. They needed plug and play because hiring managers advanced by filling jobs quickly—not by being creative.

Steve couldn't get anywhere.

He still had no assignment. He had no control over his transfer to civilian life and no idea where he was going to work. While officially retired from the Navy, he was, in his mind, now technically unemployed for 2.5 months.

Steve began to internalize the stress. The uncertainty of where they were going to live and what he was going to do wasn't adding any value to the family.

He had to adapt quickly before he had mission failure on all fronts.

Adapt and overcome.

Sometimes people find a job that is a good fit. Everything about the job fits them—it provides meaning and purpose. This is what the Navy provided Steve.

To find that again seemed impossible.

So Steve searched to supplement his purpose. He knew that what he really loved about the Navy, besides the bright white uniforms, the comradery, and the thrills, was the opportunity to work with highly motivated young people that wanted to take on challenges.

He loved mentoring and seeing young people think through and overcome problems.

He ignored the frustrations and lack of purpose he was feeling and began investing in transitioning service members to help them understand their value and get them pointed in the right direction.

Steve wanted to help them avoid some of the roadblocks he faced and to educate them on the process of transition. As Steve was intimately aware, regardless of rank, the process of transition and finding new employment can be overwhelming.

Steve would invest hours meeting with both senior and junior ranks and help them identify their value and highlight their skills. He offered to make connections and rolled up his sleeves to help his transitioning brothers and sisters connect mission and purpose in the civilian sector.

Helping them find mission and purpose was critical in Steve's mind, even though he had yet to truly find his own next mission or purpose. He remained hopeful that he, too, would find employment that offered both mission and purpose again.

Each day he invested many hours in others with no expectation of pay. He viewed each meeting, and each coffee appointment, as a deposit in the bank of karma. And he had a circle of friends that continued to encourage him to "keep doing what he was doing" as they were certain it would pay off. Jimmy was one such friend.

And then it happened.

Steve got a call from The Informatics Applications Group (*tiag*™). The company, based out of Reston, Virginia, was leading in a number of Department of Defense projects and aside from providing expert management and technology consulting services, was known to attract and hire the best talent in the market place—and treat them like talent, not like a commodity.

They were exploring the expansion of projects in the Pacific Northwest, specifically in telehealth and technology—areas that Steve had no specific hard-skill background in. But they didn't seem to get hung up on that; they wanted someone who could understand complex systems, had senior DoD experience and understood the issues around Post Traumatic Stress in reservists.

Because of Steve's unique experience with the FTS program and his work with reservists, he understood many of the issues reservists struggled with—one of them being their apprehension to express any mental health-related concerns for fear of losing their jobs. *Tiag*™ was working to help solve this issue—and Steve knew he could be the match-maker between problem and solution.

Steve is now a senior client engagement executive with *tiag*™ and is commissioned to deploy his problem-solving aptitude and passion for public service to build new relationships that will help *tiag* solve real-world problems. His ability to think both strategically and tactically is helping the company transform mission-critical environments.

Steve found both mission and purpose again. And it was because of his willingness to adapt and overcome.

The months of unemployment and rejection weren't easy, but the experience was eye-opening.

Regardless of the mission, Steve did his research. Perhaps it had something to do with his upbringing or his commitment to being a life-long learner.

Ignorance wasn't—and still isn't—an option for anyone who wants to make it in today's world.

When veterans land at colleges or in companies, they bring not only real-world experience, but a commitment to mission—and while that commitment might lack hard-skill experience it is not a deterrent in the mind of the veteran and nor should it be for the institution or company.

If Steve wasn't the expert on a subject, he would find the expert or he'd research and gain institutional awareness on the subject. This is a trait that many veterans possess—simply because not knowing isn't an option. The only option is mission success—and whatever it takes to accomplish mission success, you do.

Change is difficult. But for those who have worn the uniform, to adapt and overcome *isn't* a cliché and it really *isn't just* a CrossFit poster—it is what they do in order to survive and succeed.

Chapter 3
PERSEVERANCE – Pressing on Regardless of Circumstances

Perseverance. Pushing through no matter the hurdle—and sometimes at whatever the cost—until one achieves the outcome he or she desires; or until there is mission failure.

When on mission, there is no time for worry. The military trains its warriors to plan each step of each mission so there's a visualized outcome—a clearly planned expectation that creates hopeful anticipation. It is common to expect a specific result based on specific actions. Practice. Drill. Rehearse. Check. Double check. Recheck. Keep doing it until whatever you are doing is second nature and gets you the result you plan for. This practice, this continual rehearsal, shapes the vision of each event and the future. And all is good. We have a clear understanding of what tomorrow brings—until we don't.

We also clearly anticipate that while we plan for 100 percent mission success, 60 percent likely will fail to go as planned. We get really good at anticipating the unplanned.

No matter how much training one goes through, a sudden shift from what we have practiced or planned requires quick thinking to shape an unknown future. There is an ever-present "wonder" or anticipation of what is going to happen during a mission when it veers from the plan, or what is going to happen when we get home from a deployment, or what life will be like after we get out of the military. Those who haven't served often panic when their career changes or when outcomes are different from expectations. The service member, however, anticipates change—after all, missions are dynamic even though we plan each step. But the rules are different outside the military. The homecoming, life after the military—none of it is ever exactly what we anticipate. You can allow yourself to panic, or you can pause and assess the situation.

How one perseveres through a situation is what sets them apart.

* * *

It's called a "pinky"—a daylight flight that lands just after sunset, but you still get credit for a night landing even though you still have daylight. These "pinkys" are not handed out often by the squadron flight officer.

Jim had just completed another successful day mission and to top it off, was getting credit for a night landing, despite there still being daylight. Pinkys sure beat "black-ass" nights—those moonless, overcast nights in the middle of the ocean that made landing on an aircraft carrier that much more difficult.

He wasn't shaking either. This was good news as many landings found Jim sitting in the cockpit, shaking. The flying was the easy part. It was the landings that were nerve-racking. Despite the years of high-quality training, numerous shore-based C-Qs, (a fancy term for Carrier Qualifications) and performing hundreds of arrested landings, Jim couldn't dump the anxiety he felt each time he approached that floating runway.

Carrier qualifications are often referred to as "hitting the boat." How you land matters. You pass CQs, you likely make it to the fleet. But the whole training experience can be frightening. Jim made it to the fleet and he was more than qualified, but hitting the boat for real without incident each time was a true art. Aviators are precision artists. Tonight, he proved he was still a true artist.

The worst intentional abuse these artists—Navy aviators—experience are arrested landings. These landings are literally a controlled crash into the deck. You go from 150 mph to zero in about two seconds. Of the four giant cables, known as the arresting gear, you hope to hook the three, which stops you from plunging off the other side of the short landing strip.

Jim sat for a moment to relish the pinky and another successful "arrest." Sometimes the landings and the missions were so intense. Not this time. This was a more relaxed landing. Good fulfilling day.

As Jim watched the sun finally set over the relatively restful sea, he began to wrestle with a big decision. Stick with his Navy brothers, satisfy his love for flying, enjoy endless comradery and relish the daily thrills that come with mission runs, or get out and take care of his family—his other love.

Blended families aren't easy and Jim had teens back home who were in crisis. He went from being a single guy with no kids to a married dad with two young kids who were now teens. Nancy, Jim's wife, was married previously to another Navy pilot who died in a training accident—and with Jim also flying, she was often anxious and anticipated the worst. His home life was in crisis.

Jim jumped from the plane and made his way across the flight deck to the galley—he'd skip the more formal wardroom this time. He could afford to be less formal. After all, he was part of just a handful of aviators who had earned a Navy Commendation medal for flying numerous missions over Iraq. He also had one for creating an outstanding data processing program. But that one seemed, well, like filler. He preferred being an ace flyer over being recognized as an ace paper pusher. Either way, he strived to be the best, regardless of the mission.

This was a good day. The tasking orders were pretty routine and the mission paid off—he got a pinky.

Jim unzipped his flight suit, exposing just the tip of his pressed undershirt, as he walked down the passageway. He reflected back on today's mission. No "telephone poles" today. Iraqis loved their surface to air missiles and when he was flying over Iraq, he was locked on by the Iraqis. Jim's warning signals sang, but Jim knew not to rely on his instruments alone. With visual flight rules this day, he could clearly see that there were no "telephone poles" sent his direction. Just a scare—but he was prepared. He was always prepared. This is what he trained for—this—and hitting targets spot on.

The flight back was uneventful. If anything, it was educational. As he flew back along the 32nd parallel he saw that Kuwaiti airfields were still intact. Numerous bombing runs had penetrated this area and it was unusual to see an airfield that looked untouched. Jim dropped to a couple thousand feet and discovered just how precise his brothers in the air were with their loads. The Iraqi revetments, a makeshift parking area for aircraft that is surrounded by blast walls on three sides so as to protect the aircraft from blasts, were hit directly. The airstrip was untouched and intact but the revetments that dotted the strip were destroyed. Absolutely no collateral damage. Jim was witnessing Navy precision—a vast improvement over WWII when collateral damage was an expected part of every mission.

This was one of Jim's last missions.

Jim got out of the Navy. He chose his personal family over his Navy family simply because he felt that picking his Navy family would be selfish. His wife and his kids needed him at home.

Many aviators choose to fly for the big airlines after military service. In most cases, flying for the airlines is a natural fit—one is already trained up with hundreds, if not thousands, of flight hours. But Jim had no interest. Jim loved flying jets, not buses, as the passenger or cargo planes are commonly known. Besides, his Navy experience didn't influence the long hours he'd have to commit as a newbie flying for the airlines. All new commercial pilots spend a ton of time flying multiple routes, which take them away from their families. If he wanted to be away from family, he'd have just stayed in the Navy.

Jim moved his family from Whidbey Island, Washington, where he was stationed, to St. Louis, Missouri in order to be closer to extended family. It wasn't long before he managed to land a corporate job in technology. Jim anticipated that he would land on his feet despite the move because of family connections and his experience. What he didn't anticipate was that he would be at least two levels behind in "corporate" experience compared to his new peers. Sure, he had officer training and eight years of flying experience. But they all had eight years of business experience.

Jim had to quickly adjust his thinking from being a hero to being a… nobody.

He loved the tech industry and the fast-paced environment, and in some ways, his new career was similar to flying jets. The people he was working with were aces in their field and the daily assignments were dynamic. He loved this part, but he knew he was definitely the newbie.

While Jim anticipated that corporate would be different than his Navy experience, he didn't anticipate being invisible when he first entered the business world. After all, he had awards and commendations and thrilling life experiences…he was a Navy aviator—one of the most prestigious positions in the Navy.

But corporate didn't really understand any of "that" life.

We've all experienced that "nobody" or "newbie" feeling at some point in our life. But for most transitioning from military service back into the civilian life, that feeling can be intensified. How does one anticipate that feeling of being a nobody when starting a new career after being at the top of one's career—even being recognized as such by the world's greatest Navy?

Some people can't handle being demoted in social status. Most anticipate a continual climb in their financial status or social standing. When change happens—whether by our own decision or unexpectedly—some choose to collect unemployment, while others do whatever it takes, even if that means starting over. They persevere.

Jim not only had to adjust his thinking, but he also had to start over. The Navy valued his input based on time served and the bars on his shoulder. He wanted to be judged by his own merits and be valued for his input and contributions every day, which is what he felt the corporate world offered. Jim, despite being a "nobody" now, was excited about the opportunity to be a contributor every day. But that was short-lived.

The thrill of corporate began to dissipate only a few months into his new job, and Jim soon found himself angry. Angry with his job, angry with his family, angry at just about everything. After some reflection, Jim realized his anger was anchored in his belief that he had lost nobility in his job. He was spending long hours at work selling technology, chasing profits and chasing shareholder value. His new boss was the shareholder.

He used to work for God and country; he used to stand ready to die for God, country, and his fellow man.

Now, he just felt greedy, shallow and materialistic. *What value is there in that?* he wondered.

His marriage—the very thing that drew him from the Navy—was still struggling, his kids were still in crisis and now he'd lost his sense of nobility.

He didn't realize how much he missed the Navy until he left. He traded brotherhood, comradery, and purpose for home-front crisis, money, and no sense of purpose.

While the money in his job was significantly greater than what he had earned as a Navy aviator, it didn't buy him a sense of purpose or solve any of the real problems at home. His life was a mess—one possibility he hadn't fully anticipated.

How does one mentally go from being a part of the country's greatest, most important mission and job to being a cog in the corporate machine with a messed up home life? For some, this can be a divide that is hard to overcome. Some drink. Some lose everything. Some take their lives.

But most don't. Most find their way to a new sense of nobility. They have a breakthrough.

After two years of emotional struggle, Jim came to grips with his situation and his new life. He could either play victim or reclaim his own sense of purpose; he knew that only he could make that decision. While he wasn't putting iron on a direct enemy anymore, he decided he would change his perspective. He would somehow find nobility in his work life, while he worked to repair his home life.

The decision was only the first step. Now he had to put action into his decision. Like any good mission, first, there is the plan and then there is the execution of the plan. It took Jim another two years to work through and discover this new sense of appreciation for his corporate job. He had to find ways to tie his new mission in with God and country, and after soul searching, Jim realized that if American business is strong, then that is a vital element in making America strong.

Jim began to find purpose in his work. Whether it was encouraging a fellow employee or laboring over profit/loss numbers and negotiations, Jim knew that every action contributed to making America strong. Some days it was tough. Office fighting, backbiting, unmet expectations, client challenges. All were worth if it meant he was continuing to do his part to make America great. He had found nobility in his work, because he found the purpose beyond the money.

Without purpose, any mission or job is mind-numbing, discouraging, and empty. It leads to burn-out. Jim adopted the attitude and belief that his purpose was to shore up America's economic strength through efficient technology and that his employer, who provided services for Fortune 1000 companies that led them to becoming more efficient, was instrumental to America's strength.

Because of Jim's contribution in technology, companies were able to streamline payroll verification processes and millions were able to make sound purchases faster. Not only was he instrumental in helping transform an industry, he now was helping people realize their American dream and grow the American economy at the same time.

He was building American innovation and strength.

He also was finding a new appreciation for being a taxpayer. While many will gripe about paying taxes, Jim came to appreciate that if one is paying taxes, one is employed. And now, he was also contributing to his first employer—the military. And it was in the military where he learned personal traits and characteristics that set him apart from more than 90 percent of Americans—a propensity for precision and excellence—and the ability to persevere. He had found nobility in actually being a taxpayer.

His commitment to excellence was paying off, too. After twelve years of serving in corporate, he had reached the executive level of his company, exceeding both the expectations and the social status of most of his peers. Jim's ability to adapt quickly, to be retrained, to exercise discipline, to maintain a single-minded focus and anticipate or foresee reactions and outcomes to decisions, catapulted him ahead of his peers and landed him in one of the corner offices.

He was changing industry, was on mission, and had found purpose. Jim was surrounded by corporate success, great friends and a supportive extended family.

And this is where most of the stories stop—at the pinnacle of success. After all, that is what most people want to read and dream about. We anticipate a happy ending.

But Jim's story, like most, was still evolving. He had all the trappings of success but his home life was still in disrepair. His marriage wasn't on the same pathway to success as his career. While his single-minded focus was propelling him to success in his job, it was failing him at his marriage. His wife wanted to move back to Washington State, and so Jim did what he was trained to do in the military—exhaust all possibilities until you have mission success or mission failure.

Jim left his successful job and moved back to Washington State to pursue success in what he deemed his most important mission—his marriage.

This sudden departure from his successful job to moving to a new environment where he knew virtually no one was part of the 60 percent of a mission that didn't go necessarily as planned. Remember, we all have a clear understanding of what tomorrow brings—until we don't.

He had planned for and anticipated a successful career, which he had achieved. But his plan for a happy marriage—the reason he left the Navy—was not yet accomplished.

So Jim did what was required. In the military one is taught that what is required to achieve success often differs from what one wants to do to be successful.

Which mindset would you rather have on your team?

He called a nationally-connected friend who ran a youth camp and asked him who he knew in the Seattle area who not only might help open some doors, but also who was completely trustworthy.

When Jim landed back in Washington State, he essentially had one point of contact, a connection he only knew through a phone call introduction.

Yet, Jim was determined he would regain mission success in his marriage and in his contribution to America—despite his "one connection."

That "one connection" led Jim to new friends and a new sense of mission and purpose. He took his industry knowledge on how to automate difficult processes and applied it to state Veterans Affairs agencies. With his help, one state agency improved their compensation and pension claims. In real speak, Jim helped one state serve more veterans because of his help and his ability to help them see the power and efficiency of automation. He also helped develop a far more robust information and resource self-service tool (VAPP, the Veterans App) to assist veterans and their families find the right resource when they needed it.

Jim was finding ways to aid and equip his fellow veterans using the skills and knowledge he had learned in corporate, backed by his military training, experience and commitment to excellence.

Once again, Jim was finding success—perhaps not financial, but certainly in purpose and impact—in his corporate life.

His new friends were grounded in Godly principles, which aided Jim in his spiritual growth. They loved to laugh and smoke cigars. It was reminiscent of his Navy brotherhood.

His marriage, though, didn't find the same success. Counseling couldn't overcome the years of hurt, pain, and misunderstandings. Old wounds resisted healing. And Jim and his wife divorced.

He had failed at this mission by most standards. No one ever sets out on any mission with the expectation or anticipation of failure. Marriage was a forever mission in his mind—and that of his spouse—until it wasn't. Some missions require a drastic adjustment—some even require aborting—something aviators are trained to do when approaches to landings are wrong or when the weather isn't right. His marriage mission was aborted.

Despite the divorce, he and his ex-wife were actually gaining a stronger appreciation for each other through friendship—something that was lost in their marriage.

So perhaps it wasn't a failure after all.

When you anticipate outcomes, do you anticipate the positive or the negative outcome? The reason the military mindset has no room for worry is simply because worry is anticipating a negative outcome.

Regardless of what you anticipate, are you willing to persevere through the moments you don't anticipate?

Jim doesn't visualize negative outcomes. He visualizes mission success, plans and trains for mission success, and exercises all necessary means to achieve mission success. And he perseveres through the times that aren't successful.

These traits are not unique to Jim, but shared amongst most who have ever served in the military. And while not all missions are successful, those who have been trained and have served in uniform learn from their failures, regroup, and find opportunity for success.

Who do you want on your team?

Chapter 4
Solution Minded

The problem-solver is one of the most valuable individuals on a team. When things get crazy, the individual who can stay clear-minded and look beyond the chaos is the go-to person. It doesn't mean this person is invincible or doesn't get shaken by events—but he does have an ability to remain calm during a crisis...or throughout life. He can fix his eyes on a problem until there is a solution—regardless of the issue.

We all know a problem-solver. This is the person who appears to have everything under control. On the surface, this person navigates with ease through whatever life throws at them. They don't appear to get rattled and they seem to view every challenge or setback as an opportunity.

This person tends to be different—not weird different, but refreshingly different. He stands out in the workplace, in the classroom, and in life. When he approaches an issue he doesn't just drop it back in your lap as something for you to solve—he comes with a solution.

The problem-solver is solution minded. He is an asset on every team—whether at home, in the classroom or in the boardroom.

Most veterans, especially those with an advanced rank, quickly learned on active duty how to become problem-solvers. They had no choice. They were trained to approach their superiors with solutions, not problems. After all, every service member is a leader in training. Leaders have solutions.

And while this may be intimidating to some, most veterans seize the opportunity.

Veterans are willing to make a decision—even when others aren't or don't. They started by raising their right hand—something that fewer than 10 percent of the country is willing to do. And sometimes that decision was made to solve a desire, an obligation or a hardship—but it is the first step on a journey to becoming solution minded.

When there is chaos or uncertainty, when others freeze because there are too many options or are fearful to make the wrong decision, the veteran will do what most won't. He will calmly offer a solution or simply solve the problem. Whether the decision is one that will impact many or just himself, he is willing to make a decision.

* * *

Chris raised his right hand, and spoke the Oath of Enlistment with confidence, "I, Chris Szarek, do solemnly swear that I will support and defend the Constitution of the United States against all enemies, foreign and domestic; that I will bear true faith and allegiance to the same; and that I will obey the orders of the President of the United States and the orders of the officers appointed over me, according to regulations and the Uniform Code of Military Justice. So help me God."

The oath was the final step after a long day at MEPS, the shortened nickname for Military Entrance Processing Station. He headed back to the hotel to get some rest. It would be the last bit of real rest he'd get for the next nine weeks. Tomorrow he would ship out for basic training where he would be instructed on leadership, physical and military training, academics, and military etiquette. His first big step to manhood.

Chris pulled the hotel comforter up and shut his eyes. This would be the last bit of luxury he would have for some time.

Chris graduated from boot camp—which not all people do—and headed off to SeaBees A School where he learned to refine his construction skills. The word "Seabee" comes from the initials "CB," which refers to the Navy's "Construction Battalion." This battalion was established in 1941 to aid the WWII war effort and was responsible for shipping large amounts of equipment and materials to the efforts across the world. More than 325,000 men served in the prestigious battalion during WWII, fighting and building on six continents and more than 300 islands. They quickly earned the reputation of taking impossible projects and making them a reality even in the middle of a battle. In the Pacific theater alone, they built 111 major airstrips and 441 piers, managed tanks for the storage of 100 million gallons of fuel, and built housing for 1.5 million men and hospitals for 70,000 patients. [viii]

Over their 70-year history they've continued to construct buildings, airstrips, roadways, and fully operational bases across the world—often in record time.

At 18 years old, Chris was honored and excited join this specialized and highly respected battalion. He also was excited he was being deployed to Rota, Spain for one of his first projects.

Naval Station Rota, also known as NAVSTA Rota, is actually a Spanish naval base commanded by a Spanish Rear Admiral and funded by the United States of America. It also happens to be a favorite duty station for most U.S. sailors. Located in the Province of Cádiz, near the town of El Puerto de Santa María, NAVSTA Rota is the largest American military community in Spain and houses U.S. Navy and U.S. Marine Corps personnel. There is a small contingent of Army and Air Force service members there as well.

Chris arrived at NAVSTA eager to get to work and eager to explore Spain. An 18-year-old in a foreign country can have a lot of fun—but the Navy wasn't founded yesterday. The work requirements were strict and the liberty—otherwise known as time off—was limited. "Fun" was typically found only one day a week, not two, like most civilian jobs.

Chris' idea of fun was getting to know the real culture of his surroundings. He wanted to get to know the people and study the architecture. He took an interest in the cobbled streets and thought about who may have walked those streets centuries ago. He wasn't like most 18-year-olds who pushed the boundaries and wasted his few free hours at the clubs. He was more of a deep thinker and tended to think through his actions and consider the outcome before he made any plans for himself.

Within a short period of time, Chris found a few guys that were a bit more tame and level headed like him, and who found the culture more fascinating than the surrounding clubs of Rota.

One afternoon, Chris and his pals hailed a taxi to El Puerto de Santa María, the neighboring town to Rota, with the intent of seeing the "real culture of Spain"—something Rota didn't offer because of the Navy's influence.

Chris discovered more than culture.

After exploring several cafes, Chris and his friends found a table at a local café—and quickly discovered they were the only Americans. Young sailors in a foreign country don't go unnoticed.

Sitting several tables away was Esther and two of her friends. They were young, impressionable, and enamored by the sailors who were adventurous enough to leave the familiarity of Rota. So they did what young girls do—they began to throw popcorn at Chris's table.

The young sailors from California responded by striking up a conversation. Before he knew it, Chris found himself enamored with Esther.

Chris now had another reason to explore the culture besides his love for architecture; his infatuation with Esther. They continued to meet when Chris could get the time off—which took planning—and sometimes just sheer coincidence. These were the days before cellphones and email.

Chris would sometimes make the trek to "The Dental Clinic," the name of the café where they first met, hoping that Esther would be waiting there. And Esther often found herself waiting for Chris, but at the café 470. Despite Chris being at The Dental Clinic and Esther at café 470, they would often find each other.

Esther found Chris to be not only handsome, but a bit goofy—and she was hooked.

The two spent as much time as they could together for the next month and half before Chris transitioned back to California. Chris was confident they would stay in touch—at least until the Gulf War hit.

Sometimes our best intentions are overwhelmed by the demands of both the urgent and events that are beyond our control. This is often when many will buckle and abandon their decision—but this also is when the problem-solver, the solution minded individual, shines.

As Chris prepared for war, he wasn't sure if he'd ever see Esther again, even though he clearly hoped he would. So he began to construct his plan to reunite. He'd find a way—as a SeaBee he learned that no project was too big and no project was impossible.

"Project reunite" proved difficult. As Chris was preparing for deployment, Desert Storm ended as quickly as it had begun. Chris figured this was his opportunity to get reassigned to Rota—and reassigned he was—to Guam.

Meanwhile, Esther wondered about Chris. She had limited American TV and watched the war unfold quickly and impressively but then end just as quickly—with no word from Chris.

Sometimes problems take time to solve. The solution minded individual knows how to discern which problems require a fast response and which require careful planning. Those who are solution-minded aren't necessarily concerned with a quick solution as he is the right solution. And, sometimes the right solution—the right outcome—is all about timing.

Two years later Chris found himself back at NAVSTA Rota hoping to reunite with Esther. It was a long shot. Chris knew that time isn't always one's friend, especially when it comes to reuniting with someone he viewed as the kindest, most attractive woman in Spain.

Chris found himself with a rare weekend off—a welcome change from the traditional one day off. He packed a small bag and set off to find Esther. No guarantees that she was still in El Puerto de Santa María, or Spain, or even single. But Chris was a SeaBee, and SeaBees didn't back down from a challenge.

He vaguely remembered how to get to her home, though he had only been there once. On his first deployment, during their month and half together, Chris and Esther had been hanging out at "The Dental Clinic" when Chris discovered he had a rip in his shorts. Esther wouldn't have it, nor could Chris really walk around the town with where the rip was, so they trekked off to her home where she lived with her family so she could sew it up.

Esther repaired the rip while Chris got to know her mom. But that was two years before. And Chris was aware that a lot can change in two years. After all, America had been at war and the Middle East had fundamentally changed.

Chris prepared himself that he may never find or see Esther again. He also prepared himself to apologize for an awkward moment should he find himself knocking on the wrong door.

Chris paused outside what he thought to be Esther's home. Two years. His mind was racing and his thoughts jumped from being confident to being anxious. Chris took a breath, and knocked. As cliché as it sounded, he convinced himself that nothing ventured, nothing gained.

The door opened.

And there stood Esther.

Chris was willing to stay the course, make a decision and carry out the steps necessary to achieve success. Had he not made the decision to explore, he knew he would always wonder and the "what if" and "if only" would haunt him forever.

Being solution-minded isn't always altruistic—sometimes it is out of self-preservation.

Esther was still single. Over the past two years both Chris and Esther had dated others but neither of them had found true love.

Stationed in Rota for another six months, Chris and Esther capitalized on each free moment to hang out with each other. And after only a month (and two years of wrestling with the what-ifs and other possibilities), Chris asked Esther to marry him. She said yes.

They exchanged vows toward the end of his deployment in Rota. He was 21 and she was 18.

Chris and Esther, now newly married, headed to California. Esther put her dream and plans to become an English teacher on hold. She left behind everything she knew in order to follow Chris. Culture, family, friends. And Chris, who was still with his unit, was preparing for yet another deployment.

The move to California was proving to be tougher than she expected. Everything in California was different from Spain. The city where they now lived was a nice area with little crime, but expensive. The architecture was different, the people were far from relaxed, the food tasted foreign and processed—even the bread tasted different.

Esther also missed her independence. In Spain she had walked everywhere. But her new home in Oxnard, California was not conducive to walking. She also had no driver's license, which made her almost totally dependent on Chris to take her where she needed to go—and he was rarely available.

In a span of less than a year, she went from being single and independent to married, fully dependent, and not really understanding her new culture and environment.

It would have been easy to give up—to go back to what was comfortable. A decision can always be changed—and it's enticing to do so especially if it reverses what is uncomfortable. But there is no growth in moving backwards.

So Esther pressed in and learned to reinvent herself. This was the beginning of becoming solution-minded.

Chris and Esther decided it was best that she move in with Chris' parents in Washington State so she was at least with family during his next deployment. Neither wanted Esther to be alone in California either—especially since she was in unfamiliar territory.

Chris sailed off in one direction and Esther moved in with the in-laws. But instead of just sitting back waiting for his return, she invested a significant amount of time improving their situation.

She didn't want to be a burden on Chris—though he never once considered her to be such—so she took a driver's education course and earned her driver's license. She then purchased her first car and decided to contribute financially as well by landing her first job. Because she and Chris left Spain before she was able to complete high school, with the support of family and with Chris being away, she completed her GED.

All in nine months.

We can choose to be victims of our circumstances or we can choose to find solutions.

It wasn't long before Esther got the hang of military life. With Chris being in the Navy, he was constantly deploying and she was constantly reinventing herself.

They soon found themselves at Naval Air Station Whidbey Island—at least they were in the same state as Chris' parents.

As Chris continued to advance in rank and responsibility, Esther decided to continue on with her education and earned her associate's degree. This was a promising step and both she and Chris were confident this was the step necessary for her to land a promising job.

What Esther discovered is that jobs for military spouses aren't always that promising. Despite her associate's degree, Esther struggled to land work. Employers were hesitant to hire her because of the uncertainty of when she would move again. But she didn't give up—and she did land a job, at a Mexican restaurant. Customers loved her as did management and she was beginning to settle in when Chris broke the news: They were being transferred again. This time to Naples, Italy.

The adventure never stopped.

She quickly learned that her associate's degree didn't carry as much weight as she expected it might. But she pressed on and landed what most would consider a step up from the Mexican restaurant. She was hired by the Navy Exchange—the Navy's version of a Target.

The jobs she was landing with her degree were falling far short of her expectations. So she decided to chase her dream.

While in Naples, Esther decided she would work toward her goal of becoming an English teacher, but that decision was quickly influenced by her trip to the Vatican. She became enamored by the stories and rich history told through art. Being in Italy—especially Naples—widened her horizons. Sure, Spain had history, but none like what she had seen at the Vatican and throughout Italy. Art was her new interest, so she changed from pursuing English to Humanities.

Chris was proving himself within the battalion and was being assigned new responsibilities and new projects—each one requiring more thought. He wasn't digging ditches anymore. He was overseeing large projects with short deadlines, tight budgets, and complicated floor plans. For Chris, life was good. He had the woman of his dreams, always knew there was a next assignment and a next deployment. He happily followed the path the Navy set before him. For Esther, she was forging new paths with each assignment and relocation—her path was far from set.

And good thing. Once again Chris was being transferred—back to Port Hueneme, Oxnard, California where they started.

This time, opportunity did come calling for Esther. She was hired as an office assistant and they quickly recognized her talent and was soon handling the Teachers' Gala for all of Ventura County. This was a big step up from the Navy Exchange. Suddenly she was coordinating a major event that had high publicity and she was making powerful connections throughout the county. After eight years of moves, forging new relationships, finding part-time jobs that tested her ego, she had a breakthrough.

Finally. They could finally breathe a bit easier. They had two solid sources of income, Esther was in her element and Chris was tracking along the Navy's plan for his advancement.

Unlike most of the other services, sailors are frequently deployed even during peace time. The SeaBees always had something to build, a new roadway to construct, or some problem to solve with an existing structure. They never stopped.

Chris received orders to Naples and Esther was once again on her own. But this time, Esther had a network of support and a job that was satisfying.

Chris shipped out and soon discovered that his orders back to Naples were lost. But the Navy always finds a way to use their assets and Chris was soon in Rota, Spain where he was now slotted to take on a big project. Esther and Chris laughed. Their life had so many interesting journeys that this would just add to the tale.

But on September 11, 2001, everything changed. Esther watched in horror as the Twin Towers collapsed and chaos erupted throughout the world. Chris wasn't by her side as the U.S. was pulled into yet another war.

It was flashbacks of Desert Storm. Chris was gone and she was alone in the states. No cell phones and all forms of communication were muted and restricted. For the first few days she wasn't sure if he was going to deploy to the war zone or not.

Fortunately for Chris and Esther, his battalion was to remain in Spain, where he was now permanently assigned. So Esther wrapped up her affairs in Port Hueneme and joined Chris back in Spain in August of 2002

Constant change. Those who serve this country and their families that serve with them develop an uncanny skill to make decisions—often with limited information or time—and then work like heck to make sure it becomes the right decision. The military family is forced to become solution-minded in order to survive. It's not that they are smarter or have some alien super-power, they just have more opportunities to exercise an ability most possess, but never have an opportunity to prove.

Chris' last tour was with the state department, which sent him to Havana, Cuba. Chris had proved his abilities and was the only Seabee assigned to Havana. They arrived in February of 2006 and because they had some time to plan for this assignment, Esther, who was bilingual, had a job lined up to interview refugees who wished to enter the U.S. Esther had managed to finish her degree at University, which proved to help in landing this job so quickly in Havana. For 10 months she worked with hopeful Cubans, determining who was a candidate for a new life. She soon applied for the Consulate position and landed the job.

She now was answering letters from Congressmen on visa cases and overseeing five staff. This was a tremendous leap from where she started—as a waitress at a Mexican restaurant. All because she was willing to find solutions to their need for more income and her desire to contribute. She didn't sit back.

Esther was passionate about her work and it showed. She was giving speeches in front of diplomats, interacting with Congressmen, and impacting lives. She was finally flourishing and was confident that when they landed back in the States she would land a great job—especially with the letters of recommendation she had.

Chris retired in 2009 and unbeknownst to them, it was one of the worst times in history to retire. They had no idea of the financial impact and fallout that was taking place. While in Cuba they had no TV and what news they did receive didn't share the whole story.

But to Chris and Esther, the situation didn't matter. They were sure they were hirable—after all, everyone was hiring veterans.

Chris was offered a job in Washington D.C. because of his diplomatic security experience and top-secret clearance. He also had managed to earn his associate's degree in between and even during deployments. But he and Esther both wanted to go back home to Washington State. They had their residency there and both felt it was time to settle, buy a home, get new friends and find jobs that didn't send them across the world.

So Chris passed on the D.C. offer and he and Esther landed in Washington State in April of 2009 without a care in the world. Esther had her bachelor's degree, an impressive resume, and letters of recommendation from top level, very influential individuals. And Chris was confident that with his security clearance and 20 plus years of working his way through some pretty tough construction projects, he would land a job quickly as well.

But it was 2009. The worst economic crash since the Great Depression. Regardless, Esther started applying to all the jobs she thought she was qualified for—big companies to government agencies. Nothing. No calls. No emails. Nothing.

Chris was facing the very same issues. He had never been out of work since he was 18 years old and now faced the worst of feelings—that no one valued his skills, trainings or abilities. His history of handling major construction projects got him nowhere—especially since the economy was at a halt. Everything around them was crashing—and Chris couldn't even get a job selling shoes.

Since they had no form of employment, just Chris's retirement, they found themselves back in the home of Chris' parents. This was not how they had envisioned their life after the military—couch surfing with mom and dad after serving in the world's greatest Navy and being a consulate.

Esther decided to abandon the search for a high-profile job and started applying to local schools—she had her degree, impressive skills and recommendations and was hopeful she could land at least a teacher's aide position. She finally got a call.

A local school came across Esther's resume and they had an opening for an entry-level job making 50 percent less than what she was accustomed to. She was back to being an office assistant. But what Esther had learned over the years was that not all solutions to current problems were ideal or perfect—sometimes the only solution is one that provides temporary relief to an immediate problem. Five months being unemployed made taking the less-than-ideal position a good, temporary solution.

Chris, though, was still struggling. He was beginning to lose his sense of purpose and had yet to find a new identity or place in the civilian world. Chris wondered if it were his communications skills that were lacking—after all, who wouldn't want him on their team? He had a resume full of achievements and commendations and worldly experience, but civilian employers didn't understand what any of it meant and he didn't know how to communicate it.

Esther helped him translate his experience into civilian speak in hopes this would turn heads. But Chris's luck or fortune wasn't changing. Each day he became more convinced that while everyone said they wanted to hire veterans, they simply didn't understand veterans so they didn't actually hire them; and Chris was certain he didn't understand the civilian sector.

Give up. Or press on. We all come to a crossroads in our life. And the decision we make at that crossroad can impact our family, our friends, and future generations. Those who serve understand clearly the impact a decision can make. Decisions in the military aren't casual—they have to be thought through. One has to be forward thinking, because lives or millions of dollars are often at stake, and both are important. That training isn't forgotten when one transitions into the civilian sector—it just isn't realized by most civilians.

Chris wasn't going to give up. Esther was now the primary bread winner and he had to do something. So he went to community college.

While he already had his associate's, he was going to go after his bachelor's. It was clear an associate degree wasn't getting him the notice he had hoped.

After a year at community college he transferred to a major four-year university in the Seattle area where he completed his bachelor's. University of Washington has an impressive business network and Chris was again confident that with his UW degree, his 20 years of military experience, his clearances and commendations, he'd be a prime candidate.

But still no calls. Application after application fell into a black hole. Chris talked to his professors, asking what he could do or how he could improve, but academic knowledge and suggestions failed to get Chris any job. So he applied to MBA school and was accepted.

Esther continued to support and encourage Chris. He was doing all the right things, but there was no confirmation that his decisions were the right ones. Esther was at least working and Chris was still searching, but he was slowly giving up. His identity was tied to his work—and he had no work.

Esther came across a job opening at the community college where Chris had attended prior to transferring. Edmonds Community College was in need of a locksmith. Yes. A locksmith. Chris winced. All his background, all his experience, all his successes and his reward was to apply as a locksmith?

Esther reminded him that she too had to start over—that over the past 20 years she was continually reinventing herself—and that this wasn't a time for ego. This was a time to be solution-minded. They needed him to work if they ever wanted to buy their own home.

Chris landed an interview—one of the few interviews he managed to land over the past three years. His interview panel was made up of veterans and while Chris was impressively over-qualified, those on the hiring panel knew his value and what impact he could make to the campus overall. He at least stood a chance. So he hoped.

It had been three years since Chris had retired. And despite his efforts to find a job, any job, whether it was scrubbing toilets or managing construction projects, he had been unsuccessful. So, he didn't have high hopes that he'd land the job at the community college—even though it was just a locksmith job.

The call came several days later. They were impressed with Chris's background. They offered him the job—and Chris was ecstatic. He was going to be the most educated campus locksmith in history—at least, that's what he told himself. The thrill of working again, of being valued, was a tremendous boost to his confidence and to his relationship with Esther.

He sold out to the mission at hand. If there were no doors to fix, he'd help the custodian. If the custodian didn't need help, he'd help the grounds keeping staff. He even helped the janitor—and always with a smile.

At night, Chris put on his suit and tie and went off to business school. He was surrounded by professionals from all industries who were getting their MBAs—they'd talk about their acquisitions, or mergers, or planes—and Chris would talk about unclogging toilets, or working on a door.

He didn't care. He was grateful. And so was Esther. Chris was finding a bounce in his step once again.

Chris graduated and now really was the most educated campus locksmith. While earning his MBA was a great achievement, he was still fixing locks, toilets, and lights. And, occasionally, he got a change of pace and found himself painting over graffiti. Esther continued to be an encourager.

Chris continued applying for jobs and networking. But when you get out of the military, you don't really have a group to call upon. And because the past three years he was in school, he didn't really have time, outside of other students, to develop a solid, professional network.

He began to struggle with his lot in life. He still wasn't getting return calls. Both he and Esther had always found a way to get back on top. They never stopped pursuing excellence in their life or the betterment of their education, but now Chris, armed with a communications degree and an MBA, was working as a locksmith, and Esther—a former consulate with her college degree was a low-level office assistant.

At what point does one accept the outcome of his decision when it doesn't result in the desired outcome? Do you press on? Do you give up? Or do you become content, but never satisfied? It differs for every individual. But what is common for most who wear the uniform is that mission above self is most important. And there is great satisfaction in being others-focused.

That was the breaking point. Or, more accurately, the breakthrough point. Chris decided to be content. At first he was concerned he was disappointing family and friends because he wasn't living up to his full potential, or to his MBA degree, but he learned to tell his friends that if this is what life had for him, he accepted it.

And he did. He embraced his life as the happy-go-lucky, highly educated campus locksmith.

But the story doesn't end here. Every decision we make sets in motion behind-the-scenes events we have no visibility or awareness of. It's for this very reason veterans think through their decisions. Because when you make a decision, you also own the decision.

One afternoon Chris was fixing an extinguisher in one of the campus tunnels when his cell phone rang. Chris answered. One of the jobs he applied for months back was for the Director of the veterans' resource center on campus. They wanted to interview him. He was thrilled. He now had an interview he really wanted. He was about to call Esther to share the news, when his phone rang again; Chris answered anticipating it was campus HR, except it wasn't campus HR. It was Human Resources, but from a large government agency that Chris also had applied to months back, and they, too, wanted to interview Chris.

Two calls, two amazing opportunities—all in a 5-minute span—shortly after deciding to be content, but not satisfied.

Chris ultimately ended up becoming the Director of the Veterans Resource Center at Edmonds Community College. He felt strongly about helping veterans and this position gave him the best platform to do so. He was confident he could build something that would benefit his fellow veterans. He helped kick off the campus Boots-to-Books campaign that raised one million dollars specifically for veterans' services and needs on campus. He established a veteran's sanctuary on campus and later discovered it was because of that sanctuary a veteran chose to get help and not commit suicide.

Chris never gave up. He knew that giving up was not a solution. It was an excuse. And when those in the civilian sector recognize that most veterans won't give up, America will be the better for it.

Esther didn't give up either. She was eventually promoted from office assistant to a secretary's job at the school and took night classes to get a degree in teaching. Today, Esther is no longer a secretary—she is now an English teacher—her original dream.

Twenty-four years and a lifetime of experience later and despite the circumstances and shortfalls, Chris and Esther both believed that America was, and still is, the land of opportunity. When the dream is big, the circumstances don't matter. And every problem does have a solution.

What America needs are more individuals who have the scar tissue and the experience to be solution-minded.

Chapter 5
OPTIMISM AND FAITH –
Always Means Always

The Marine Corps has a reputation for being America's force in readiness. Always prepared to fight, anywhere, at any time. They take boys and chisel them into modern-day Spartans. And now, they do the same with women.

One can argue that a trained Marine is a true optimist. At least when it comes to ability.

An optimist believes that what they are about to take on, whether it is business or mission-related, will turn out well. There is not a Marine on the planet who thinks otherwise. They train to get positive results. Every time. Always.

They also have faith. And faith is built on trust—an assurance that what they believe, when put to the test, will net or deliver the result they expect. They have faith in their ability. They have faith in those in their unit and they have faith in their command. Many even have faith in God.

But to the outside world, a Marine may seem skeptical or pessimistic. Maybe even rigid and unbending. Often, marines are known to question those they don't trust and they don't trust blindly. They trust what they know and their motto, Semper Fidelis—"always faithful"—is an absolute. It is a mindset.

But many Americans today don't like absolutes. Grey is the new acceptable color to describe where we stand on issues or values—no more black and white. Besides, one can't really be "always" anything, can they? Look at America—we celebrate almost everything that is anything but absolute. No wonder we struggle with being optimistic—and why our faith in anything bigger than our own selves is wavering. Absolute is no longer an American value.

But it should be. We as Americans should be absolute in our belief and desire to make America shine. This starts with trust. We, as Americans, should be able to trust our government, trust our leaders, and trust those we work with—but trust is based on honesty. Similarly, integrity should be an absolute.

And, it is for many of our veterans. Integrity is an absolute. A commitment to strong moral principles and a belief that our words have value and should be anchored in truth is deep in the fiber of our military. It is why many start out optimistic. It becomes a fiber that runs through every veteran worth his salt.

America should embrace integrity—because then she'll see optimism and faith blossom. And when a veteran, who is still holding on to optimism and faith, becomes a part of your team, it will change the fiber of your organization.

Developing true optimism and faith often comes at a cost that many civilians are not willing to pay. Steel is forged under pressure and intense heat as were many of our veterans. And it is because of these intense experiences they become great leaders.

America needs leaders who have true optimism and faith.

* * *

Marine Corps Second Lieutenant Ilario Pantano answered the phone. It was Lieutenant General James Mattis, commanding general of the 1st Marine Division. "Congratulations, Lieutenant Pantano, on being exonerated and cleared of all charges. We need Marines like you. I am offering you command of a unit that is preparing to deploy to Afghanistan." Ilario paused, took a deep breath, "Sir, thank you. But I respectfully resign my commission."

These aren't the exact words, but they do describe the scenario. Ilario Pantano had been to hell and back and was now being offered command of another unit. The gesture was a sign of trust in his abilities and his leadership. But he knew it was time. Time to move on to the next assignment. He wasn't going to assume command of another unit, but on the other hand, he sure as hell wasn't going to quit.

Marines never quit. They get reassigned. And after the death threats, being brought up on charges that would have had him on death row, and carrying burdens that weren't his, Ilario was reassigning himself—and the first step was resigning his commission as a Second Lieutenant in the United States Marine Corps.

His optimism and faith had been stretched. But the boy who grew up in the Hell's Kitchen neighborhood of Manhattan was still confident he could make something out of all the chaos. He'd always made something out of every situation he was in from the moment he walked into the recruiter's office in 1989.

He was 17 when he first said yes to the Marine Corps. It was his ticket out of Hell's Kitchen and he was sure he could make a difference in the country's premiere fighting force. Great leaders were forged in the Marines and he was determined to become a great leader.

As he was pushed to new limits in boot camp, Ilario watched the Berlin wall come down and hoped that he would be able to contribute to some event that would be just as significant. At 17, most young men dream of being part of something that is the catalyst for great change. Little did Ilario know, he would have his opportunity.

He became a TOW gunner, which is the guy behind the tripod-mounted anti-tank missile assault weapon. The TOW, which stands for Tube-launched, Optically tracked, Wire-guided, is one of the most widely used anti-tank guided missile weapons in the military. The anti-tank missilemen, as they are commonly called, provide medium and heavy anti-armor fire in support of the infantry battalion. Throughout America's modern-day conflict, the men behind these weapons tend to see action—a lot of action.

In August of 1990, Saddam Hussein, the dictator of Iraq, decided he wanted to expand his control of the Middle East and ordered his army into the neighboring country of Kuwait. At one point, Iraq, during its eight-year war with Iran, was a beneficiary of the United States' military aid; giving them impressive weaponry and helping them establish the fourth largest army in the world. So when Saddam's army rolled into Kuwait, it was coming well equipped with the intent of a takeover.

Saddam Hussein's hostile actions posed a major threat to the world's oil supply. If he was able to gain control of Kuwait and move his way into Saudi Arabia, Iraq would control one-fifth of the world's oil. And world leaders, even Iraq's supposed ally, the USSR, was uncomfortable with this potential outcome.[ix]

Opportunity knocked. Ilario was about to become a part of something big. Every Marine knew he was about to go to war. But as a newly minted Marine, one who had only recently completed his TOW course at Infantry Training Battalion, School of Infantry, Ilario had no idea what war would really look like.

In the last months of 1990, President George H.W. Bush ordered more than 500,000 troops into Saudi Arabia to defend the Saudis against a potential Iraqi invasion in what became known as Operation Desert Shield. He also issued an ultimatum to the Iraqi Dictator to leave Kuwait by January 15, 1991 or face a massive attack by a multinational force.

Saddam ignored the ultimatum. And Ilario found himself crossing into Iraq under huge plumes of oil smoke, so thick that if one left a pen on a white sheet of paper for just a moment, it would cast a white outline when removed – and would fade within moments only to be covered by the oil-filled smoke.

It was a terrifying experience. War is never anything but terrifying— but for Ilario, it was short-lived. Within weeks, the U.S. and its multinational allies had more than overwhelmed Saddam and his Iraqi army with their superior fighting forces. Within 72 hours of stepping into Iraq, Ilario was back in Kuwait watching Saddam and his forces retreat from Desert Storm.

While many of Ilario's fellow warfighters recovered and the U.S. celebrated its domination over an evil dictator, Ilario applied to the U.S. Marine Corps Scout Sniper School and was accepted.

To be a USMC Scout Sniper, Ilario had to become highly skilled in marksmanship and fieldcraft. He would learn not only how to deliver long-range precision fire on selected targets from concealed positions, but he would learn how and where to hide, how to quickly memorize battlefield details, infiltration and escape routes, and enemy force doctrines and equipment. He became an elite stealth fighter.

Upon completion of sniper school, Ilario was promoted to Sergeant and assigned to a commando unit where he again took part in operations that didn't always make the headlines. He participated in Operation Provide Promise, a little-known humanitarian relief operation in Bosnia and Herzegovina during the Yugoslav Wars. While he cycled out before the completion of that operation, it went on to become known as the longest running humanitarian airlift in history. Ilario had once again been a part of a world-changing event.

His efforts and his training, as well as the missions he had been assigned, fueled his optimism and faith. Or maybe it was his cockiness and ego. Optimism and faith, prior to being truly tested, is often born from cockiness and ego. And there was no question that Ilario believed there was nothing he couldn't do and he had the ego to back him up, no matter what it was.

Ilario left the Marines to attend college back in his home state of New York. The boy from Hell's Kitchen was returning to familiar territory as a salty and seasoned combat veteran. He landed a job as a security guard at the Hard Rock Café in New York City while he attended New York University. Here he honed his people skills, learning to put on the charm and greet people with a smile, while remaining observant at one of the most popular and busiest restaurants in Time Square. Having been a sniper in wartime, he was interesting and marketable in the field of security, which is why he was able to land the Time Square job so quickly.

But it became evident rather quickly that most civilians at his university didn't understand him or what he did, or the significance and sacrifices made because of war. Desert Storm required nothing of the civilian population and was essentially over before most Americans understood what was going on. Ilario understood why some couldn't understand his sacrifice. But when a student in his class failed to know the significance of December 7, 1941, a frustrated Ilario packed his bag and walked out of the class.

How could America be great if its educators didn't teach the lessons learned from events that changed the world?

Ilario continued to go to class, but he was now clearly aware that most college kids didn't understand veterans. And, it didn't stop at the students. His exposure to everyday civilians at the restaurant, while positive, made it clear that most Americans went about their lives with little to no understanding of the sacrifices made to keep the country and its interests safe.

Regardless of the ignorance he witnessed, Ilario didn't allow that to cloud his interest and commitment to make a difference or to finish his degree. In just three years Ilario had managed to complete college and, because of the connections he was able to make through his job and his military experience, land a job as a clerk on the floor of the commodity exchange with Goldman Sachs.

His dedication to excellence and his confidence in his own ability to achieve success soon landed him on the trading floor—as an energy trader. From infantry to energy. Ilario's confidence continued to grow and his training to evaluate and make decisions quickly was a tremendous asset.

From 1995 to 1998, he was a member of the start-up team that integrated the top-tier investment bank culture with the utility business through Constellation Power, an electricity trading joint venture that was eventually acquired for $11 billion.

He was making quick decisions that had real consequences. But when rolling blackouts were hitting California and impacting the lives of hundreds of thousands, all while he and his team were celebrating because of the money they were making, it hit him.

This wasn't him. He wanted to make people happy and not make money from people's misery. He left to join the world of entertainment.

Ilario was experiencing what most great leaders experience: a transformation from self to selfless and from profit-focused to purpose-focused. It's not that purpose and profit can't coexist—they can and should. But what Ilario was beginning to feel is that when one is driven by something bigger than themselves, all the money in the world won't make a difference.

He soon became a movie producer with the New York-based firm The Shooting Gallery, which had a few hits, and also co-founded Filter Media, a company specializing in design and interactive television. Ilario loved the fast-paced environment of media as well as being an impact player in the emergence of on-demand and SMS technology through television. He was soon working with big companies like Mattel, Cablevision and Sony.

His personal life was thriving as well. Ilario found a soulmate in Jill Chapman, who happened to be a successful entrepreneur as well as a fashion model, and the two were married in 1999.

He was on top of the world.

Until September 11, 2001.

His world went to hell. As he approached 5th Avenue and 23rd St., Ilario could see the Twin Towers burning a mile away. Millions of shimmering pieces of paper were floating around the Towers and the Manhattan skyline. To Ilario, it looked like a million angels had descended on New York. But this attack was pure evil.

Always faithful. A Marine never quits and when duty calls, or America cries, a true warrior answers the call.

Once again, Ilario knew America was at war. He pulled over, found the nearest barber, got a high and tight haircut, pulled his gear out of storage and, on September 12, was actively working to get back into the Marine Corps.

America had not been assaulted to this scale since December 7, 1941, and, as a result, men and women of all ages were volunteering to serve.

His eagerness to go was getting bottlenecked by age waivers, family waivers, and buried enlistment records. As the weeks passed, Ilario was fighting both anger and sadness as he dealt with the death of friends, including one of the first men who, years ago, gave him a job right out of Marine Corps. The building where he had worked while at Goldman Sachs, 4 World Trade Center, was destroyed in the attacks as was a fire station, where eleven fireman, four of whom were Marines, perished.

But there he sat, on the sidelines. For three months he jumped through hoops, but the process for re-enlistment was proving to be too slow. So he applied to Officer Candidate School and was accepted.

While Ilario poured over the books and trained at OCS, the U.S. government had determined that Saddam Hussein was a colluder in the attacks on America and in March of 2003, the invasion of Iraq commenced with Shock and Awe—a military term used to describe the use of overwhelming power and shear force dominance over one's enemy.

Days before Ilario graduated at the top of his class and was commissioned as a Second Lieutenant, the 2nd Marine Expeditionary Brigade was engaged in a fierce fight with Iraqi forces as it came to the aid of a U.S. Army supply convoy from the 507th Maintenance Company. The convoy had mistakenly taken a wrong turn and ventured deep into enemy-held territory and came under attack. For more than five days the battle raged between U.S. forces and Iraqis, and the casualties mounted. The Marines were able to rescue 10 soldiers of the 507th, but the ambush took the lives of 11 soldiers in what became known as The Battle of Nasiriyah.

On the very same day The Battle of Nasiriyah commenced, March 23, 2003, 18 men of Charlie Company, 1st Battalion, 2nd Marines, were killed around Saddam Canal. This became the bloodiest day of operations for the Marines.

Ilario was convinced that he would change the outcome of the war, but he had to get there first.

He finished Infantry officer course in December of 2003 and was assigned to the 2nd Battalion, 2nd Marines—known as the Warlords—in February 2004.

As his battalion was in transit to Iraq that same month, Saddam was finally caught, and Ilario—as did many of his brothers—thought the war was over. The Warlords were greeted by an unusually quiet February.

But leaders are proactive. They very rarely sit and wait for things to happen. Their optimism drives them to seek out ways to continually improve. And many veterans gain this trait.

Ilario used the time to conduct training drills in an effort to better prepare his men, and while some of his men grumbled, they understood the why behind his motivation. He believed the more they trained, the fitter they were, the more likely they all would survive a real war. His confidence, which anchored his platoon's trust, along with his concern for each one of his men, made him popular not only among his platoon, but also with his superiors.

Little did he know how important this would be in the coming months.

While Ilario trained his men throughout the month of March, the insurgency had been building quietly behind the scenes. Saddam was gone, but the fight was far from over.

Four U.S. contractors were ambushed, brutally killed, and their bodies hung from a bridge in Fallujah for all the world to see. This was at the end of March.

While many Iraqis took to the streets in celebration, Ilario and his men raged, and Americans wanted justice. The city of Fallujah was barricaded in by U.S. forces and The First Battle of Fallujah, also known as Operation Vigilant Resolve, commenced to root out the perpetrators who committed the heinous act.

Extensive ground troop operations were conducted while jets dropped bombs. Ilario's commitment to training his men was paying off. In more than 40 combat operations, his platoon suffered one casualty—a shrapnel nick from incoming mortar.

Others weren't so fortunate. The I Marine Expeditionary Force (MEF), which had deployed to Anbar in March 2004 as part of Multi-National Force West to carry out stability and reconstruction operations, had lost 27 Marines and 90 more casualties.

In just the first few days of April, more U.S. troops were killed than the previous eight months combined. It was a devastating month—and it wasn't over; but Ilario was committed to seeing this trend reverse.

His optimism that all would turn out well and that he could change the course of the war was anchored in his training and his ability to lead men. He was certain that his platoon of America's chiseled warriors would root out the evil. He had faith in not only his men, but also in his abilities.

Aggressive measures were deployed to find and bring the men responsible for the killings to justice, but the media, instead of focusing on the atrocities carried out against U.S. forces was instead highlighting the accusations of excessive force by U.S. troops. Political pressure forced the hand of the U.S. government and the hunt for these killers was suspended. This added to a heightened sensitivity to the rules of engagement.[x]

Every action and every decision were being scrutinized and questioned. But Ilario didn't mind—he knew his actions and his decisions were for the betterment of his men and the mission. His team knew him to be firm, but fair and had adopted the saying, "No better friend, no worse enemy."[xi]

Those were true words for Ilario. And those words were about to play out in an unexpected way.

On April 15, 2004, acting on information extracted from captured insurgents, Ilario led his platoon against a compound near the town of Mahmudiyah. As his platoon approached the compound, it saw a vehicle speeding off. Ilario ordered his men to stop the vehicle and to have the occupants of the vehicle handcuffed. Ilario stayed with the captives and proceeded to have the vehicle searched for weapons, while the rest of his platoon secured the compound.

His men found the compound deserted, but it did have a cache of arms, including "several mortar aiming stakes, a flare gun, three AK47 rifles, 10 AK magazines with assault vests and IED making material. [xii]

Concerned there may be other insurgents coming, Ilario posted two men on watch, removed the ties from the Iraqis' wrists and ordered them to search the vehicle again.

All decisions have outcomes—some have consequences. And some consequences will test even the strongest person's resolve, optimism and faith.

As the Iraqis were ordered to search the vehicle, Ilario became acutely aware of their small talk and believed they were conspiring together. His years as a sniper had trained him to observe even the smallest details. While the Iraqis had revealed no weapons yet, that certainly didn't mean they weren't there. After all, with what was found in the compound, it was likely the vehicle was harboring weapons. And with the death count mounting over the past few days—on all sides—Ilario wanted no surprises. He was watching closely.

The two Iraqis turned to face each other and Ilario shouted, "Stop!" in both Arabic and English. They didn't stop. And Ilario made a split second decision that changed his life.

Ilario shot the two Iraqi captives.

Killing the enemy is expected in combat. Murder is not.

One of his Marines, whom Ilario had previously demoted and who was assigned forward watch, registered a complaint about the incident, triggering a Naval Criminal Investigation Service (NCIS) probe.

Ilario soon found himself making national headlines, but for all the wrong reasons. He was being accused of premeditated murder.

On February 1, 2005, Ilario was charged with two counts of premeditated murder, and faced the death penalty if convicted.

The once invincible, popular officer now faced an Article 32, a proceeding under the United States Uniform Code of Military Justice, similar to that of a preliminary hearing in civilian law. If the hearing revealed that Ilario was in violation of the UCMJ, he would then be prosecuted at a Court Martial—where only the most serious cases are heard.

The charges were without merit, but that didn't stop the proceedings. In light of Abu Ghraib, where personnel of both the U.S. Army and the Central Intelligence Agency committed a series of human rights violations against detainees, the investigation into the charges would be thorough.

The national news covered parts of the trial, exposing only the accusations that drove ratings, and not the heroism of this beloved Marine. A site in Pakistan displayed an image of Ilario being beheaded in retaliation for his supposed crime, and his family began receiving death threats.

But through it all, Ilario stood firm in his resolve. His optimism and faith were being tested along the way, but when your life is built on integrity, he knew he could stand firm in his convictions.

The accuser was found to be guilty of bringing forward false charges and read his rights while on the stand. Ilario was found to be not guilty—and fully exonerated.

But the experience was traumatic, not only on Ilario, but his entire family. And so, he respectfully turned down one of the most revered Marine Corps Generals in recent times and reassigned himself.

He went back to North Carolina where he and his wife had moved shortly after 9/11, and became a sheriff's deputy. Shortly after, he received a book deal from Simon & Schuster to tell his story and while at home recalling the events of the past few months and years, his battalion went back to Iraq and 15 Marines lost their lives. The guilt of not being with them—typically referred to as survivor's guilt—compounded his pain. He found himself in a very dark place.

On June 12, 2006, Ilario's autobiographical account of his experiences, Warlord: No Better Friend, No Worse Enemy, was released and he soon found himself making the promotion rounds, even appearing on The Daily Show. But the notoriety and the publicity failed to bring him any comfort.

Ilario falsely had believed he could have saved those men who had died while he was back in the comforts of his own home writing about his experience. He was his own god, capable—in his own mind—of changing the outcome of that incident and the war.

His optimism and faith were a false front for what was really his cockiness and ego—which were draining him of his will to live.

When Chris, a soldier who had been in his unit when he was on active duty, committed suicide, Ilario was consumed with guilt and grief and began shutting off the world. He stopped corresponding to loved ones—and stopped answering his phone.

The fact that he had a beautiful wife and two beautiful children was not enough to keep him grounded. His optimism and faith were falsely anchored in cockiness and ego—he was descending into hell.

Ilario worked out religiously at a CrossFit gym, attempting to refocus his emotional pain on pushing himself physically. His life was a wreck, though, from all appearances, he was on top of the world. Great family, a successful book deal, deputy sheriff.

He managed to muster the energy to develop a relationship with an individual who also worked out at the gym. Ilario was impressed by his character and how he treated his family. His new friend was a good dad… something Ilario wanted to be himself. He hadn't met many men like this in the civilian world and so they quickly became workout partners.

His partner began to share how true optimism and faith weren't built on self, but on Christ. But Ilario didn't want to hear it. He pushed him away, but his partner was persistent—a trait Ilario respected and was familiar with. So Ilario, the chiseled Marine covered in tattoos who was struggling to find value in life, challenged him. But it wasn't a challenge of physical strength or wits—he challenged his workout partner's grace.

Ilario was convinced that when people got to know what he was accused of, they would run. So he challenged his friend to Google him. And so he did.

The articles his friend read didn't discourage him one bit nor did the articles stop him from wanting to develop a relationship with the Marine who was once headed to death row.

Ilario was moved by his kindness, his grace, and his character, and was ultimately saved, both literally and figuratively, by turning his life over to Christ. He began to understand the true foundation of optimism and faith and how they are anchored in God, not self. It became evident to him that God had always been present—through all the trials, the painful moments, the grief, and even the victories. God was that still small voice that ultimately prevented Ilario from taking the same path as his friend Chris.

Soon after, Ilario was blessed with scholarships to attend grad school and found himself heavily involved in politics—eventually running for a U.S. Representative seat for North Carolina. The race was close, but instead of heading to Washington, D.C. he was selected to be the Director of Veterans Affairs in North Carolina.

In 10 years' time, Ilario went from being a Second Lieutenant facing death row to being in charge of a state department that oversaw the care for over 800,000 veterans. And, while the journey wasn't easy, he doesn't regret one minute.

Ilario's experience and battle scars prepared him to fight for other Marines and other veterans who faced challenges, whether those challenges were personal or brought about by a system hell-bent on making it difficult.

As Director of VA in North Carolina, he was instrumental in helping cut veteran unemployment in the state by 50 percent. When he started, the state also had no Veteran Courts—special courts specifically geared toward hearing veteran cases and taking into consideration the veteran's history and experience when considering the judgment; the state now has three.

He developed one of the most comprehensive resource guides in the country and worked with other agencies to attract jobs that ultimately attract veterans. During his tenure, jobs, education, and training for veterans have all improved. Ilario knows that when a state focuses on education and employment opportunities, the emotional stresses are reduced, which in turn reduces a number of other challenges.

His optimism and faith are now anchored in Christ and not self; his integrity is absolute.

Ilario's scars drove him to change himself and allowed him to change a state. Out of the pain came good. And today he is a walking testament of his favorite verse, Romans 8:28: "And we know that in all things God works for the good of those who love him, who have been called according to his purpose."

This is the optimist leader. The veteran, who regardless of the trial or challenge, stands back up after being knocked down, and says, "Send me. I will go. I will be the one who stands in the gap."

Industry needs this leader.

Chapter 6
LOYALTY – Understanding Support and Allegiance

Loyalty. A devotion and faithfulness to a country, organization, or an individual that is so strong, it can't be broken. Our government wants loyalty, industry wants loyalty, and most people want loyalty.

But what does loyalty look like?

When government, or industry, or individuals talk of loyalty it is often framed in nostalgia, confined to the history books and part of days long past. To be loyal is often thought of as being old fashioned or shortsighted, or worse yet, foolish. After all, in order to succeed, one must "get their own" and look out for themselves. Loyalty only stands in the way of that happening.

This could be the reason fewer than one percent of Americans commit to the United States to serve without conditions. These one percenters subject themselves to a new set of rules because they are devoted to preserving what this country stands for—no matter the cost. It's not about them.

When other nations fold or other armies desert, U.S. forces stand strong. When the men and women transition and face bureaucratic red tape and delays in benefits and services, they don't lose their pride in the country.

Regardless of the uniform that was worn, if one served, he or she is family and will come to the aid of a brother or sister in need.

That is loyalty.

Granted, loyalty doesn't always start in the purist form. Sometimes is starts out of self-preservation—like getting a job because one needs the money, but then falling in love with the company or organization because of its mission or impact.

Regardless of how it starts, when loyalty has matured, it is stronger than steel.

America's greatest asset possesses loyalty. The real question is: Are you worthy of their loyalty?

* * *

Everyone has options—and choices. Jovita found herself with two options: stay in Indiana and continue to associate in her current circles, and likely become pregnant, because that seemed to be the pathway most 18-year-olds took in her neighborhood, or, join the military and pursue a life she knew nothing about. The choice seemed clear: The only way out for her was to join the Army.

Her decision to join had nothing to do with loyalty to a cause or a mission. It was a way out of an environment she no longer wanted to endure. Her decision was simply a pathway forward.

She became a Food Service Specialist, learning how to prepare, cook, and serve food in the field and on base. For an 18-year-old from her part of Indiana, this was a welcome change. Many of her friends had opted to stay behind and weren't making much of their lives. Here, she was able to meet people from across the country, have at least three square meals a day, was clothed, and was building some great friendships…and she had a purpose. She played an important role—keeping the warfighters fed.

Sure, some occupations in life don't appear glamorous, but they are 100 percent necessary. Mission above self. Jovita was thrilled she could serve the needs of the military, and she knew she was adding value.

In 1996, while stationed at Fort Bragg, North Carolina, Jovita took notice of a young private who stood out among the crowd of many green uniforms. She asked her girlfriends if they knew who the soldier was, but to them he was a mystery. But she was determined to meet this private, known only as Fenwick.

Dan Fenwick was a 20-year-old who hailed from Maryland. Young, fit, and with a big smile, he, like Jovita, wanted a new start in life and having few options, chose to join the military. In reality, it was his last ditch effort to get out of Maryland and change his life.

For weeks Jovita kept an eye on Dan when he paid a visit to her chow hall. She'd flash a smile and managed to get his attention on occasion, but she hesitated to do anything too bold. If there was one thing she was learning from the military, it was that one must learn to stretch outside their comfort zone if she ever were to advance.

Jovita made her move. She finally introduced herself to the man she had been noticing. For Jovita it was a step in the right direction and a bold move on her part, but worth it. Dan finally knew who she was and was glad for it.

One afternoon, Dan and Jovita casually bumped into each other at the gym. Now to casually bump into anyone at Fort Bragg takes planning. Fort Bragg is one of the largest Army installations in the world and home to the XVIII Airborne Corps, 82nd Airborne Division, and the U.S. Army Special Operations Command. It covers close to 251 square miles and is home to close to 40,000 soldiers and support staff. There are few coincidences at Fort Bragg.

Dan, having just watched the movie Rocky, decided to steal a scene from the movie and asked Jovita is she'd like to go ice skating. It worked for Rocky and he was hoping it would work for him, too. It did.

Two young, penniless privates found themselves laughing and having a good time on the ice and closed the night out at their favorite restaurant, Taco Bell.

Three years and two kids later, Dan and Jovita got married. It was an unconventional start to their relationship and their journey to discovering the true meaning of loyalty.

Shortly after their wedding, Dan—or Fenwick as he was commonly referred—received orders to Fort Campbell, home to the 101st Airborne Division and the 160th Special Operations Aviation Regiment. Jovita did not.

While the Army has a program called The Married Army Couples Program, which provides the opportunity for a married couple to be assigned together, it does not guarantee an assignment together. Simply put, just because two individuals are married to each other in the military doesn't mean they'll be stationed or living together. The mission of the military comes before the marriage of the couple. The Fenwicks, as they both were called now, were quickly learning that above all else, the military expects your loyalty.

Dan fought to get Jovita reassigned and she was finally able to join him at Fort Campbell after three long months. Dan wasn't a fan of the separation—being away from Jovita and his two young children was difficult; and knowing that Jovita was tasked with not only performing her required duties, but also caring for their kids when she got off work, didn't sit well with Dan. It didn't sit well with Jovita either. The demands of work and caring for two young children without Dan were trying. They both welcomed the reunion.

Fort Campbell was decades newer than Fort Bragg, as it was established in the 1940s and not the early years at the turn of the century. Aside from The Sabalauski Air Assault School, where courses in Air Assault, Pathfinder, Pre-Ranger, Jumpmaster Refresher, and Rappel Master are taught, Fort Campbell is known for its full-time parachute team, known as the "Screaming Eagles." Dan knew his time at Fort Campbell could very well be cool and interesting.

As the Fenwicks began to settle and get a routine in order, the United States was attacked. They watched with horror as two planes steered into the Twin Towers and created havoc throughout the country. Every soldier was put on alert, and Jovita, who was assigned to Special Operations Command as support, was shipped out on the first rotation, leaving Dan at home with their two young children.

Loyalty isn't always convenient. As a matter of fact, it can be straight up inconvenient. And two opposing schedules can—and do—break even the strongest of couples. With the Fenwicks being newly married, they were being put to the test.

Dan managed. If Jovita could manage, he could manage. They were Fenwicks, and they began to speak strength into who they were and what they wanted to stand for. Separation wouldn't break them; they would just have to figure it out.

Dan's duties as an Air Assault Instructor were demanding and, with Jovita being deployed, he knew he needed help with the kids. The base had childcare, but the hours didn't always align with his long hours so he started shepherding the kids to friends—and sometimes to friends of friends. The kids, while not fully aware, were being exposed to the true meaning of extended family. No matter what, someone was there to help—even though they weren't blood related.

The kids bounced around for close to six months while Jovita was deployed to Iraq and Dan was shouldering the up-tempo of training and instructing. America was essentially at war and while it was expected that those in uniform do whatever it took to ensure mission success, there was an unspoken expectation that the children of those who served would do the same.

For Dan and Jovita's young children, that meant accepting the many faces who came into their lives while mom and dad supported the mission.

Both Dan and the children welcomed Jovita's return in early 2002 and soon after, Jovita and Dan discovered they were pregnant again. The six-month separation turned into a growth opportunity, not only in their emotional abilities to handle the stress of the unknown and the demands of the mission, but also in their family.

The two young children still had to shuffle around despite Jovita's return. She was a soldier first, then a mother in the eyes of the Army. And while the Army, like all branches, does a tremendous job of supporting military families, they are in the business of protecting and defending the interests of the United States, and not changing the mission requirements to support the needs of the family. Jovita was just as busy as Dan upon her return, despite being pregnant.

The Fenwicks welcomed their third child into their Fort Campbell family; and only after a few months of spending time with the newest member of his family, Dan and his team were deployed to Iraq. Jovita was back to being a single mom, now with two young children, a newborn, and a demanding work schedule.

Loyalty isn't easy. People want it, but it requires work and can be demanding. The military provides opportunity—mental and physical training, steady income, a skill, lessons in leadership, and purpose—in exchange for loyalty. Some can handle the demands, some cannot.

Jovita had parting news for Dan—they were pregnant again. Only two months after the birth of their third child. Dan and Jovita had developed a bit of a reputation, not only for being in a fast-family expansion mode, but for being able to handle it. No matter what "it" was. The Fenwicks would handle this demand, too.

There was no doubt in either of their minds that these were character-building moments. But they were also moments to display how ready, willing, and able they were to handle whatever came their way. Dan deployed for six months and, like most deployments to Iraq, it was harrowing. In 2003, the fighting was intense and the casualties high. The media coverage was more thorough than it had been in previous conflicts, but misreporting of troop casualties, while infrequent, would cause angst and worry back at the home front. Fortunately for Jovita, she and Dan were able to talk occasionally, and even when it got messy or the uncertainty was overwhelming, she had a strong support network and very understanding supervisors.

Despite the constant revolving door of responsibility, the long-distance relationship, three kids and being pregnant, the Fenwicks were more ambitious than they were tired. They loved the Army, they loved each other and they were loyal to both.

When Dan returned, they received orders to their next assignment. So they packed up, said their goodbyes, loaded up all four kids, and shipped out...to Italy.

Italy is a dream assignment except when the U.S. is at war. No matter where one was assigned, he or she was subject to being deployed to a war zone. No sooner had they received housing that Dan got the word that he had to prepare for Afghanistan. Iraq was being handled and Afghanistan needed to be handled—and his team would be one of the teams handling it. Touring Italy would have to wait.

Four kids in a foreign country, Dan and Jovita not knowing the language—at all—and Jovita preparing to once again be a single, yet working mom with a husband in a combat zone.

The Fenwick 6, as they referred to themselves, knew they could handle it. They took it one day at a time, and did whatever it took to get through the day.

The next year wasn't easy. Both Dan and Jovita faced heavy demands. Dan and his team as part of an Airborne artillery unit, would drop into some pretty tough areas and it was Dan's responsibility to ensure that all his men came home. He had to devote 100 percent of his energy, focus, and loyalty to the mission at hand. To do otherwise would risk injury or death—he had no time for distractions.

Jovita knew this. Distractions of any kind could lead to mission distractions. And mission distractions led to flag-covered boxes. She kept Dan informed but only at a high level. She didn't have time for much else anyway. This was a time before most soldiers had cellphones, so when she was able to hear Dan's voice, it was because he had access to a Satellite phone. She protected him from knowing about the constant fights with daycare or having to deal with their son being kicked out school. She wouldn't share that each time they hung up the phone she would cry not only because she missed him but out of exhaustion. What was the point? Dan couldn't help anyway, so she kept it light.

Besides, she didn't need him to worry. So she did what she needed to do every day. One day at a time. She would get up, put on her uniform, shepherd the kids to multiple locations, deal with whatever trials the kids drummed up, and still perform her job with excellence.

Loyalty demands excellence. Not perfection—that's not achievable. But excellence is. Excellence is the quality or trait or standard that surpasses expectations. It requires a commitment to remove excuses.

She was a Fenwick. Fenwicks strived for excellence in all they did. And that commitment was one of the reasons she and Dan both continued to advance in rank. So, she removed the excuses and did whatever it took. She was loyal to the family name and to the mission.

As soon as Dan stepped off the plane, he learned that his whole unit was being relocated to Germany. So once again, they packed up, Jovita said her goodbyes, shipped their cars, and proceeded to get acquainted with new schools, new housing and another new language.

They barely got settled when they both received orders to Afghanistan. It wasn't a change of duty station, so now they had to figure out what they were going to do with the Fenwick 4…their kids. They knew no one in Germany and finding someone who was going to watch their kids during their deployment wasn't an Army problem.

Jovita phoned her sister back in Indiana who agreed to help, even though she had never met the kids, nor raised kids of her own.

Loyalty will drive someone to do what most won't.

Dan and Jovita and their four kids, 11, 8, 5, and 4, boarded a plane— at their own expense—and made the long journey to Indiana. The kids had never met their extended family and the schools they were to attend had little to no experience with military families nor an understanding of the issues the kids might experience. The community as a whole only knew what the media told them about the Wars on Terror. They were dropping their kids off in uncertain territory. Sure, they trusted family, but it was the lack of understanding as a whole that caused concern. But Dan and Jovita didn't have time to ease the hand off for their children. Duty called.

They were doing what most people wouldn't.

Dan and Jovita arrived back in Germany and promptly deployed to Afghanistan for 15 months. Dan made it clear that he and Jovita were never to work together, or even in the same proximity, while in a combat zone. This carried over to traveling as well. His experience had taught him that it was better that he and Jovita be separated even if deployed in the same zone just to preserve one of them in the event all hell broke loose.

Their loyalty to country had both of them away from their children— and from each other for most of those 15 months. Dan and Jovita did manage to see each other on occasion since they both were in Afghanistan, but they were sure to keep the visits short to ensure their kids didn't wind up orphans.

Halfway in to the deployment, Jovita received an urgent call from her sister. Her sister was overwhelmed. Having never had kids, and now having four, was too much. So Jovita made arrangements with her mom to take the kids and instructed her sister to take the Fenwick 4 to grandma's house. The kids had never met grandma and were just getting settled into their new schools. But that didn't matter. The kids were packed up and taken to new schools in a new city to live with a relative they didn't even know. What the kids did know is that their extended family was much different than their military family.

Shortly after the kids settled into grandma's, Dan and Jovita were up for R & R—the military's acronym for Rest and Relaxation. Dan and Jovita flew from Afghanistan back to Indiana; on separate planes. It was a long-awaited for reunion. The Fenwick 6 was reunited.

In a matter of 12 years, Dan and Jovita had gone from newlyweds with two kids, to trained warriors with four kids, who were jumping between war zones, different duty stations in other countries and shipping their kids off to friends they knew, friends they didn't know and now to family who didn't even know how to raise kids.

Loyalty doesn't have a timeline or expiration date, unless there is a violation of that loyalty. But the Army had yet to violate anything—they had only provided opportunity—and with opportunity came expectations.

Jovita was considering her exit. She had given a good 12 years and with Dan's continual deployments, as well as hers, and being separated from the kids, the thought of leaving the uniform to head back to the civilian world where there was more routine was appealing.

But that thought was short-lived. Dan flew back to Afghanistan to complete his tour and as Jovita was preparing to do the same, she received notice that her application had been reviewed and she had been selected to attend Warrant Officer Candidate School. Go or no go?

To serve the Army as a Warrant Officer is an honor. Candidates are typically selected from the enlistment ranks because of their commitment to excellence. Should she choose to attend, as a candidate, she would be immersed in training that would transform the individual into an officer who "is a leader of character committed to doing what is right legally, morally, and ethically both on or off duty."[xiii]

This was Jovita already, but to serve in the world's greatest Army as a Warrant Officer, and to hone her skills and leadership abilities was more appealing than the routine of civilian life.

So the Fenwick 4 stayed with grandma as Jovita jetted back to Germany to pack up their home and ship their cars back to the states before she headed off to Fort Rucker, Alabama, to become a Warrant Officer in the U.S. Army.

After graduating Warrant Officer Candidate School, she was off to attend Warrant Officer Basic Course at Fort Lee, Virginia where she was provided the technical training necessary to certify her as technically and tactically competent to serve in her designated occupation—food service and commissary. She knew the food service world well having been exposed to all the behind-the-scenes on set-up, logistics, and delivery while being in theater. The multiple deployments overseas, both in Italy and Germany, also provided her knowledge and expertise that came in handy while attending the Basic Course.

She was more than ready to be put in charge of more than just the food service line. And she was more than ready to see her kids.

Meanwhile, Dan was still finishing up his tour in Afghanistan. The months were dragging on, the days were long, and the separation from his family grueling. He wanted to be home. He was getting tired.

Jovita was able to call Dan and inform him that she had graduated and their new orders were taking them to Fort Bliss, Texas, the Army's second-largest installation, covering an area of more than 1,700 square miles with a footprint that rests in both New Mexico and Texas.

Once again Jovita was tasked with packing up the home front while Dan was deployed. She raced from Fort Lee, Virginia to Indiana, packed up the minivan, loaded the four kids and the dog, and drove for three days to El Paso, Texas.

The constant moves and the separations were getting tough. Being loyal to a demanding organization or individual, regardless of its altruism or motives, can wear down even the strongest person. But this is when true loyalty is revealed.

Jovita's new role as a Warrant Officer and Dan's role as a senior non-commissioned officer made the Fenwicks a power couple, but not just because of their ranks. Over the years they had worked to create an image that they could do and handle all things. To their subordinates and peers, they were the couple that smiled through every challenge. After all, many people knew of the rotations, the long deployments, the farming out of their four kids. When most couples splintered, the Fenwicks held their ground. They were fighters. They held on to this image and the name they had created. But still, all this was held together by only the slightest thread.

Exhausted but grateful to be alive, Dan rolled into Fort Bliss after completing his 15-month tour in Afghanistan. A lot had happened during that time. His kids were moved back and forth across Indiana, Jovita had graduated from Warrant Officer School, and they were now in Texas. Germany was a distant memory. Fort Bliss could be the sanctuary where they all needed to get refueled.

Dan was now tasked with operations at Fort Bliss, which allowed him a more regular schedule, but like most services, a regular schedule is a moving target. At least he was home. And good thing. Jovita was called up to Iraq—it was her turn. Dan would now be assuming the duties and tasks of homemaker and of engaged parent for the next 12 months while Jovita was away from her family. Would it ever stop?

Dan and Jovita were struggling under the smiles. From 2004 through 2007, their kids had attended five different elementary schools, were traded back and forth between friends and family, and lived in three different countries. When Dan would pull in from an assignment, Jovita would head out the door for hers. Their lives were in constant upheaval. They were doing what most Americas won't; they were making sacrifices most Americans don't; and they were barely hanging on while most of America sat safely at home watching reality TV.

Did their loyalty matter?

By 2010, the Fenwick ego was buckling under the weight of responsibilities and upheaval. When Jovita returned from her 12-month deployment, she went seeking something bigger than their ego and found herself sitting in a church pew. Dan figured Jovita needed that more than he did—after all, they were Fenwicks. They looked good, they smelled good, they were a power couple with a great name. The Fenwick 6 could get through anything…and Dan didn't want or need one more thing to "attend."

But their unhappiness was proving to be an aggressive enemy. All the sacrifices, all the challenges and the emotional pressures were too much. They couldn't hide behind the smiles anymore. They wanted out; and Jovita wanted Dan out. So Dan packed.

Dan and Jovita were breaking. Certainly people would understand if they got a divorce. After all, they had enough evidence to prove that they had overcome more than most so if everything fell apart, they'd still have their pride and ego. Besides, no one really expected them to get through what they'd been through and make it out the other side. And the kids would survive—they were still young and had become accustomed to mom and dad being away from each other more than they were together; it would somehow all work out.

One can only be so loyal, right?

But that wasn't the Fenwick way. Dan called Jovita and suggested they call the church. He was willing to try anything to preserve the Fenwick 6. His ego was on the line. Their name was on the line—and, truth be told, he didn't want to lose what they had built. They had invested and sacrificed way too much over the years to let it all go without a fight.

The church was receptive to their call, even though Dan had not really been a participant. The church instructed them to come back in two weeks and Dan promptly informed the church that his marriage didn't have two weeks.

How hard will you fight to hold on to something you believe in?

They met with the Pastor the next day. True loyalty is often forged through overcoming a crisis—together—and the pastor knew this. He also knew that he was dealing with a couple that was holding on to an image when they should be fighting for substance. The pastor spoke truth—the Fenwick 6 needed something bigger than themselves if they were going to survive this. If they wanted to know true loyalty, they had to stretch beyond their family and the Army. They had to learn to trust something bigger.

Dan and Jovita both started reading the Bible and regularly attending church. Over the years they had been surrounded by great communities, a great military family, and had some stellar professional mentors that had helped them navigate their careers. But what they needed now were personal mentors that could help them navigate their marriage and shore up the Fenwick 6.

The decision to be loyal to each other, to fight for their family, was working. They started pulling their marriage back together and found renewed hope in having a personal relationship with God. They were no longer going to embrace Edging God Out.

Dan chose to retire two years later in 2012. As a Sergeant First Class, he was able to look back over his time and see the impact he had made. They were solid years of dedication and commitment. The Army had provided opportunities and experiences he never would have had had he chosen to stay in Maryland. But the temporary separation from Jovita and the meetings with the pastor revealed that everything he received from the military—the most important being his family—he was about to lose because of the military. He was resetting his priorities.

Jovita received orders to Joint Base Lewis McChord in Washington State and the Fenwick 6 once again packed up, but this time was different. Because of the separation and the decision to fight and preserve what they had—and the decision to bring God along, the move wasn't as traumatic. The Fenwicks really could do anything and they could do it now because their confidence was no longer rooted in image and ego.

Dan and Jovita also viewed this assignment as the first step in their next mission: to help other couples succeed in their marriages. They both were convinced that society spends far more time talking about the wedding when it should be more focused on what happens after the wedding. The wedding day is magical, but the days and years after the wedding can erase all that magic if there isn't more focus put on the daily life.

Dan and Jovita today are both retired from the Army and their personal mission to invest in and walk side-by-side with other couples continues to grow. They are building an army of couples who understands that marriage can be wonderful and fun and that traditions can be developed regardless of the trials and circumstances. After all, the Fenwick 6—yes, even their children—are convinced that if they can survive, others can too.

They are an example of true loyalty. A devotion and faithfulness to a country, organization, or an individual that is so strong it can't be broken. And there are many others like them. A great majority of our veterans have learned what it means to be loyal. They fight for what they believe in and they fight for each other. They fight for what is right and true.

Dan and Jovita today are loyal to their family and to their marriage because they are loyal to their country. Their journey wasn't easy, but being loyal isn't always easy.

Many veterans today understand the true meaning of loyalty.

But the real question remains: does America or industry deserve their loyalty?

Chapter 7
VALUES – The Foundation
for America's Greatness

American values. At one point in history, when this was spoken of, people understood the truths inherent behind what was being said. Freedom, family, God, truth, happiness, equality, democracy, and champion of the little guy, were just a few of the values that came to mind. For some, it was as simple as God, country and apple pie.

But now, American values seems to mean whatever a political party or activist group wants it to mean. Even the word "values"—if spoken by the "wrong" organization—can set off a media firestorm or a small-town riot.

Every young man and woman who joins the military quickly learns that there are a standard set of values they will be subscribing to. These standard values are the foundation on which that branch rests. It is how order and expectations are managed. Loyalty, Duty, Respect, Selfless Service, Honor, Integrity, and Personal Courage aren't just words for those in the Army—it is what every U.S. Army soldier is about.

The Air Force's core values of Integrity first, Service before self, and Excellence in all they do provide excellent guideposts on how to conduct both their professional military lives as well as their personal lives.[xiv]

The Coast Guard, an often forgotten branch of our services, subscribes to Honor, Respect, and Devotion to duty; it is the compass that guides their mission to defend and preserve the United States of America from both internal and external threats, natural and man-made.

And then there are the Navy core values, of which every Marine adopts as well since they are a branch of the Navy. These bedrock principles consist of three basic principles:

Honor: "I will bear true faith and allegiance..." Accordingly, every Sailor and Marine will: Conduct [themselves] in the highest ethical manner in all relationships with peers, superiors and subordinates.

Courage: "I will support and defend..." Accordingly, every Sailor and Marine will have: courage to meet the demands of [their] profession and the mission when it is hazardous, demanding, or otherwise difficult.

Commitment: "I will obey the orders..." Accordingly, every Sailor and Marine will: Demand respect up and down the chain of command; Care for the safety, professional, personal and spiritual well-being of [their] people; Show respect toward all people without regard to race, religion, or gender; Treat each individual with human dignity.

These defined standards—or values—are what shape and define the members of each service. And it is these values that allow our military to operate with little confusion—even when these men and women are from different branches doing joint operations.

When our military men and women transition into the civilian world, they most often are introduced to a civilian world that is operating without any standard values system. There are no uniforms to indicate what values one prescribes to in the civilian sector. Each individual can claim his or her values are the right values and if one disagrees, it is a sign of hate or disregard, or discrimination. Everyone's values are right...even when they contradict in the civilian world. There is no foundation for American values.

There's no mystery why there is so much confusion, frustration, and even protests in today's America.

But all is not lost.

Today's veteran brings stability to his surroundings. He or she brings a sense of strength, confidence and know-how. This isn't true because they are better than others, it simply is because they have a foundation and know their values are tried and true.

Core values remove confusion. And today's industries and campuses—and America as a whole—could use a lot less confusion.

* * *

Honor. Courage. Commitment. The Navy way. Standards that Tim was about to embrace as he prepared to head off to boot camp in 1990. A native of Seattle, Washington, Tim decided to enlist in the United States Navy to seek new adventure and a career.

After graduating Boot Camp in Orlando, Florida, Tim attended Hospitalman, a school in Great Lakes, Illinois where he learned the skills and knowledge required to serve as a primary medical caregiver for sailors. His occupation as a Corpsman would allow him to serve in a variety of capacities and locations, including naval hospitals and clinics or aboard ships. It would provide variety. After all, everyone needs medical care at some point.

Instead of racing off to the fleet or some shore assignment, Tim went to Basic Underwater Demolition SEAL school—BUD/S for short. Established by President John F. Kennedy in 1962, the Navy's Sea, Air and Land Forces—commonly known as SEALs—are expertly trained to deliver highly specialized, intensely challenging warfare capabilities that are beyond the means of standard military forces. They are an elite group of men who achieve the impossible by way of critical thinking, sheer willpower and absolute dedication to their training, their missions and their fellow Special Operations team members.[xv]

However, before one can actually pin on the Trident, he has to graduate from BUD/S. Preparation consists of more than 12 months of training that includes Basic Underwater Demolition/SEAL BUD/S School, Parachute Jump School and SEAL Qualification Training (SQT), followed by months of pre-deployment training and intensive specialized training.

It is grueling.

But before the obstacle courses, it starts with learning the values of teamwork and mental perseverance. Candidates must show humility and integrity throughout the process. Honor, Courage, and Commitment are tested at every level and when one makes it through the training, those traits become engrained.

Many don't make it and Drop On Request (DOR). They ring the brass bell three times, pack their bags and await their fate in the fleet.

Not Tim. Tim was determined and finally graduated—class 182— in 1992. He then went on to attend Joint Special Operations Medical Training 18D and was assigned to SEAL Team 8 as a SEAL Corpsman.

His desire for adventure and purpose was fully underway.

He completed several worldwide combat deployments before he was assigned to the Naval Special Warfare Center in Coronado, California. In just a short time, he was returning from where he graduated to become a SEAL instructor.

From student to instructor in just a short period of time.

As he shaped new minds and pushed men to new impossible limits, he met Liz. Little did he know that Liz would soon be the secret to his success. Tim and Liz hit it off and were soon spending as many free moments together as they could. It didn't take long for them to know they were made for each other.

His training had conditioned him to believe that nothing was impossible and that all things are achievable. With Liz by his side as his strongest supporter and encourager, Tim earned his Bachelor of Science in Psychology from Regents College while still serving as a SEAL instructor. Liz and Tim also got married.

When one operates from a fixed foundation, there is security. While surroundings and events can seem chaotic, knowing what you stand for, knowing your support, and knowing that what you believe in is tried and true brings calm.

Liz entered the teaching field while Tim continued to advance in his career and soon found herself traversing across the country as they went from Coronado to Fort Sam in Houston, Texas. She, too, was building up her own resiliency and finding that there was great strength in knowing the values they both subscribed to. Amongst the moves, the demanding schedules and the constant change, knowing that she and Tim shared common values brought comfort when life was chaotic.

Tim and Liz both leveraged their off hours by continuing to pursue education. In January 2002, he graduated from the Interservice Physician Assistant Program with a Bachelor's of Science in Physician Assistant Studies from the University of Nebraska and Liz graduated from San Diego State University with her Master's of Education. Tim was commissioned shortly after as an Ensign in the United States Navy and, in 2003, he earned a Master's of Physician Assistant Studies with an emphasis in Family Practice from the University of Nebraska.

Shared values and a shared commitment to excellence and improving themselves was their recipe for early success.

In addition to his educational achievements, Tim went from enlisted to officer ranks within just a few short years.

Tim wasn't defined by his education, rank or even the fact that he was a highly regarded SEAL—part of the military's elite. Sure, all those contributed to his standing in the military, but he was, in many ways, instead defined by his values. Both he and Liz were. They applied Honor, Courage, and Commitment to all areas of their lives because it removed confusion and allowed them both to press into life—they had a value system in which to filter their life. And that filter helped them make better decisions.

It was good they did. Being a Navy SEAL and the spouse of a Navy SEAL isn't just glamour, tight shorts, and formal events. It comes with a lot of stress and anxiety. Every mission can be the last mission. Every phone call could be the phone call that delivers bad news. Silence during a deployment can be both good—and bad.

While in Baghdad, Tim and his team were caught in an operation that went south. Liz, meanwhile, was at home recovering from a miscarriage. Life was coming down hard on them as a couple and individually. Tim managed to call Liz from a SAT phone, despite being wounded, to inform her that he would be okay. And Liz, while lunching with fellow teachers, had to muster a voice of encouragement while hearing gunfire in the background.

Being stressed doesn't properly describe all the struggling feelings inside.

When life comes down hard on couples, many break. They break because their relationship isn't anchored in shared beliefs or values. The crises cause such a divide that the bridge required to connect them is too vast—and they remain divided forever. This too can happen inside industries, organizations and even governments. When vision and values aren't shared, chaos erupts, and the outcome isn't good.

Fortunately for Tim and Liz, they knew where they mustered their strength. They leaned on each other, their values, and their belief in God to get them through.

Liz had developed a tenacity that was unshakable. Traveling across the country, dealing with uncertainty during Tim's deployments, and having to periodically readjust to build a new life every couple of years had strengthened Liz's resolve. Raising their family wasn't easy. Their marriage wasn't easy either. But most marriages aren't. Liz knew her marriage to Tim would present more difficult moments than non-military marriages, but she took an oath. Both she and Tim took an oath—to each other and to country. That oath committed them to something greater than themselves. They chose to "embrace the suck" and learned to talk through the difficult moments.

They were a team. And as every member in the military learns, teams are designed to get each other through the difficult moments. What starts as a team, finishes as a team. No man is left behind.

Tim and Liz were committed to making sure that philosophy would apply to their marriage and to their children, regardless.

They rebounded from their medical issues and, over the years, Tim continued to serve in a number of leadership positions that took them to Great Lakes, Illinois; Camp Lejune in North Carolina; and to Stuttgart,

Germany. While Liz was proving to be committed to mission success in her personal and professional life, she was learning that most of her civilian associates were not. It was becoming more and more apparent that those who did not share the values she and Tim shared, or have their training or had committed to something bigger than themselves, were being absorbed by self-interests. And self-interests often lead to conflict—her profession was losing sight of the mission, which was to achieve excellence in education.

Liz was fighting professional battles on the home front. Fellow teachers failed to grasp the importance of the bigger picture and would quarrel over issues because of individual needs and desires instead of valuing individual sacrifice for mission success. Her workplace life was nowhere near the life she appreciated inside her military family. She didn't know who her friend was or who her enemy was. They could have very well been the same person on different days.

Selfishness was gaining ground on selflessness.

To Liz, this was a foreign belief system. The reason missions succeed in the military is because of a selfless view—a desire or need to accomplish something bigger than personal gain. Failing to have a team view limits one's success. But team view can only be achieved if there are shared values and a common vision.

Liz was seeing common vision and values slowly erode in her professional environment. Tim only knew of men and women who believed in mission above self.

In February of 2016, Tim retired after receiving a favorable offer in the civilian world. He struggled over the decision to re-enlist or reassign himself. The Navy had been good to him. Over his 25-year career, he had amassed a number of personal achievements and awards including the Bronze Star with Valor, Meritorious Service Medal, Navy and Marine Corps Commendations Medal (5), Navy and Marine Corps Achievement Medal (2) and various campaign medals and unit citations. The young man who ventured into the Navy in 1990 was leaving after becoming a SEAL, Fleet Marine Force Officer (FMF), and a Dive Medical Officer (DMO) to focus on being a better husband to Liz and a better father to their three children. He was looking forward to testing his skills, talents and abilities in the civilian market place.

But the civilian marketplace is different from the military. Tim quickly learned that honor, courage and commitment were foreign words to the young team he was tasked with managing. His team members would show up late, and when they did show up, they had little interest in working. They would question everything and if it got too tough, they would just quit. They were committed to nothing—except maybe whatever pleased them.

Tim was shocked. The men he served with were never late and the only way to do a job was to do it with excellence. Training had taught him and the rest of his crew that when the mission leader gave a command, you followed immediately because it not only could very well save your life, but it would certainly be to the benefit of the mission. And no one quits. A team member does not quit on his team.

When Tim brought the challenge—along with potential solutions—to his boss, the quick response was, "Welcome to the real world," and that was followed by a quick lecture educating him that what he was taught and what he learned while in the military didn't apply to the civilian sector.

Liz, too, was finding with her new life outside the military. They no longer knew whom they could trust. Loyalty and dedication were hard to find among their civilian counterparts.

Industry without shared core values will not survive. Its teams will splinter under the weight of conflict and confusion. The same goes not only for our communities, but also this country.

For Tim and Liz, the difference between those who serve in the military and those who don't is glaring. And they learned quickly that it had little to do with education and everything to do with values.

Traits like being punctual and working hard should be engrained in our youth. Selfless service, respect, integrity and courage are core values that benefit all of society and should be expected by young and old.

The statement, "I can't do it" should be challenged. America's greatest asset—the veteran—will always find a way. "Can't" is simply an indication of an unwillingness to try harder. "Can't" is not part of any veteran value system.

Those in government, in education, in corporate need to hold themselves and those they lead to a higher standard. America needs to try harder.

Tim and Liz both serve on the frontlines, but in a different capacity. Tim continues to position his leadership skills in corporate and makes himself available to those who want to understand the benefit of subscribing to proven values. Liz gives back by volunteering her time in non-profits and by sharing her experiences and providing tips to couples who desire a stronger marriage. Both have come to terms that the civilian world is much different than the military.

But neither has embraced the statement that the rudderless ways of the civilian world are "the real world."

When America embraces those like Tim and Liz, who regardless of the color of the uniform they wore, stood on principle and values, the world will once again know—and understand—what American values means.

Chapter 8
RESPECT – When American Industry Respects its Greatest Asset

Author's note: I'm breaking from the normal cadence of the book in this chapter for one primary reason; I'm about to endorse a Wall Street company. As I mentioned in my acknowledgments, when one endorses someone or something, there is risk. I'm willing to take that risk because of the impact this company is having—not only on Wall Street, but also in the lives of veterans. That being said, this chapter will be shorter than most because the point can be made rather quickly.

* * *

For years *Fortune* magazine published a list of the World's Most Admired Companies. To anyone picking up the magazine, these were the companies to work for—Wall Street admired them, analysts admired them, executives across the country admired them. To make the list was a testament to capitalism and a sought-after workplace. But the "definitive report card on corporate reputation" only considered the *Fortune* 1,000. To be considered to be admired, you first had to have the revenue.

So was it really the social responsibility or some of the other nine criteria items these companies were ranked on that actually garnered the respect? Or was the feeling of deep admiration for their achievements based mostly off of revenue and investment returns? One could argue they wouldn't have the revenue if they weren't respected. But is that where respect starts?

In the military, respect has nothing to do with money. Every day one works to earn the respect of his subordinates, peers and superiors by performing above expectations and committing without wavering to the mission at hand.

Because it is earned, respect is valued. It can take months and years to earn, yet it can be lost in a simple act of stupidity or ignorance.

So, the military guides its young men and women. Those who serve in uniform subscribe to a code of ethics, a set of standards and values that are reminders to how one should be and act, both in and out of uniform. Things like, honesty, integrity, accountability, loyalty, fairness, compassion and keeping one's word are engrained in their training and expected to be part of their character throughout their lives. These values lead to and preserve respect.

Are these the values our colleges and our corporate entities profess or teach: Honesty, integrity, accountability, loyalty, fairness, compassion…keeping one's word? Do they value respect—or just profit?

America was once one of the most respected countries in the world. This was during a time when a number of our veterans were serving in public office. Our colleges were flowing over with veterans and industry was growing rapidly because of their talent. They may not have had the skill, but they certainly had the aptitude. It was a time when America embraced her returning service members and gladly followed their lead.

Our nation and industries will once again become respected when they embrace our veterans instead of cower at or suspiciously question their experiences.

America's greatest asset is being valued at a few companies and colleges across the country. And their participation is transforming the culture and even the bottom line. The relationship is built not on pity, or tax incentive, or GI Bill dollars, but rather, on respect.

Will you follow their lead?

* * *

Respect: a feeling of deep admiration for someone or something elicited by their abilities, qualities, or achievements.

Six months into his Army deployment in Iraq, Captain Scott Smiley's life was nearly ended by a roadside bomb, causing him to go totally blind. A West Point grad, an Army Ranger with a bright career ahead and newly married to his junior high school sweetheart, his deployment to Mosul, Iraq in October 2005, changed the course of his life.

In Operation Iraqi Freedom and Operation Enduring Freedom, for every U.S. soldier killed, seven are wounded. Combined, over 48,000 servicemen and women have been physically injured in the recent military conflicts. Others experience invisible wounds.

But these physical and invisible wounds of war often don't stop the warrior while in service—or out. Many rise above it. They learn to deal with it and move on to make impact. They respect the country they serve, and so they press on out of admiration and sheer will to continue to make a difference.

After his near-death experience, Scotty spent months recovering and rehabilitating, then returning to active duty where he taught leadership and commanded a Warrior Transition Unit at West Point. He was the Army's first blind active duty officer and commander at West Point, who was also a recipient of the Purple Heart, Bronze star and the prestigious Macarthur Leadership Award.

He was the epitome of the modern day warrior's grit and resolve to overcome physical challenge—regardless of the circumstances. He had the respect of many in uniform.

But when service ends, the transition into the civilian sector for the combat veteran can be filled with uncertainty. And if one is injured, the transition can be flat-out discouraging.

Instead of being valued for their accomplishments, veterans are often scrutinized or pitied because of their experience or injuries. Questions like, how will you react if you hear loud noises from interviewers seeking to uncover some PTSD trigger point seem innocent enough, but, in fact, are asked out of fear or protection—and send a message that the veteran is misunderstood. Statements like, "What you learned in the military doesn't apply here in corporate" are uttered by ignorant corporate managers or executives who have no idea what leadership truly means and that the skills and training almost every veteran brings to the marketplace is based on time-tested, proven leadership.

And respect is often demanded in the civilian world—not earned.

And yet America wonders why the transition is so difficult—and veterans wonder why their civilian brothers and sisters have forgotten what made America strong in the first place.

Some companies do sign a pledge to hire veterans, but many of those same companies fail to capitalize on the skills, abilities, and dedication veterans bring to the market place.

But there are a few companies that stand out. One in particular—founded by someone who was part of the one percent. Not the wealthy one percent in the beginning, but the one percent that chose to wear the uniform during an ugly part of America's history—Vietnam. And now he is serving the seven percent.

Lawrence Doll, Chairman and Founder of Drexel Hamilton,[xvi] a firm he started in 2007, initially achieved success as an entrepreneur in the real estate industry. He founded both The Lawrence Doll Company, which specialized in land development, and Lawrence Doll Homes, a builder of upscale homes and townhouses. Both were proving to be lucrative and adding value. His success led him to become the Chairman of the Board of United Bank, a retail and commercial banking subsidiary of United Bankshares with more than $7 billion in assets and operations in Maryland, Virginia, and the District of Columbia. A position he still holds today.

But as a service-disabled United States Marine Corps veteran, whose duty in Vietnam earned him two Purple Hearts, the Vietnamese Cross of Gallantry, and a prestigious appointment to the United States Marine Corps Honor Guard in Washington, D.C., he wanted to do something that would honor and respect the men and women who served this country honorably.

He wanted to provide an opportunity like no other. So he founded Drexel Hamilton, a service-disabled, veteran-owned brokerage based in downtown New York with the mission of helping combat veterans gain a foothold in the financial industry upon returning to civilian life.

To be clear, he did not start it out of pity or for some tax incentive. Drexel is not a charity to give combat veterans a handout. It is a full-service Wall Street brokerage firm that is committed to making money for its clients and hard work is required.

As a Marine, Doll understood the strength in training and equipping people with the tools and knowledge they need to become a success. He also understood that if they succeeded, he would succeed.

It wasn't easy. Starting the firm in 2007 at the precipice of the major financial meltdown wasn't great timing. But like most veterans, he understood that sometimes one has to work like hell to make the decision they made into the right decision. So he did. He attracted men and women with integrity and honor, who respected both opportunity and profit. By 2010, he had amassed only 10 employees. Today, Drexel now has close to 100 employees and 39 are veterans.

More than 20 of the 39 employees are disabled veterans.

Scotty Smiley is one of those employees. Drexel Hamilton recognized and respected his talent and his work ethic. While Scotty made a name for himself on active duty, he didn't stop there. He wrote a book about his experience and, in 2015, completed a 2.4 mile swim, 112 mile bike ride and a ran a marathon in just under 17 hours—and was named an Ironman.

John Glynn, Managing Director of Corporate Trading and part of Drexel's senior management revealed why Drexel is succeeding.

"Drexel identifies the work ethic and we've found a strong work ethic in this veteran crew. Close to 90 percent of [veteran] hires have no background in the industry, [but what] they have is a strong desire to add value to clients. We've found the secret to adding value and making money."

And they do make money. Last year Drexel was involved in nearly $12.8 billion of commercial mortgage-backed securities; and that is only one of their service lines.

Their commitment and respect for veterans separates them from the rest of the Wall Street brokerage firms. They are the only service-disabled, veteran-owned financial institution named to Military Times 2016 "Best for Vets" list.

Drexel Hamilton understands something most companies miss; skill can be trained. What veterans might lack in industry know-how, they make up for in character, aptitude and work ethic. And in a short period of time, because of the training, the veteran masters the necessary skills.

There is little risk for Drexel Hamilton.

Drexel Hamilton is leveraging America's greatest asset—the U.S. veteran—and both are benefiting from the mutual respect.

Will you follow their lead?

Chapter 9
MISSION43 – How Education is Transforming a State Through Collaboration

If America is to remain strong, its citizens need to have the best education in the world—and those who educate can't be solely from the ivory towers. We need to learn from those who have real world knowledge, too.

Those who serve in the military are trained by some of the very best leaders in the world—educators who have walked the talk and can impart real-world, real-life solutions to some of the most complex problems. They are not just learning about how to fire off a weapon or drop iron; they are learning how to lead in difficult environments, how to win the hearts and minds of those they are around, and what true diversity means. Their real-world education has gained them invaluable scar tissue that is passed along to those coming up the ranks.

Indeed, the veterans' classroom has never been limited to just four walls and a whiteboard.

Gaining access to this knowledge—or maybe it is wisdom—will transform those who choose to leverage it. Whether it was Francis Bacon or Thomas Hobbes, who was secretary to Bacon as a young man, who wrote "Knowledge is Power," doesn't matter. What matters is that there is truth in the statement.

Knowledge is power and when institutions, industries, and even states decide to collaborate and pull their best minds and talent together, from all walks—warfighters to white collars—true transformation is sure to emerge.

Why? Because collaboration focuses on vision, not solely on individual interests. It removes scarcity thinking and replaces it with, "When we do this together, we all win."

Collaboration is the art of setting egos aside and working with others to create something great.

* * *

The state of Idaho is on to something great. And this is their blue print.

After our hour-long meeting, Roger, the Executive Director of the J.A. and Kathryn Albertson Family Foundation (JKAF), looked at me and asked a parting question, "If you could do one thing that would benefit veterans, what would it be?"

"One thing," I paused. Parting questions were supposed to be simple. Where does one start when it comes to doing something that would benefit veterans? Do you start at the Department of Defense and work to change their transition process so it incorporates more partnerships with industry and with Veterans Affairs? Or do you start at the Department of Veterans Affairs and work to speed up the benefits and services? Or perhaps you start with state government and help them coordinate a statewide initiative and hope it doesn't get bogged down in competing interests or bureaucratic councils?

Or do you promote your own program in hopes of getting funding?

For me, the answer was simple. "Roger, here's my one thing: I'd change the conversation around veterans. We are America's answer, not America's problem. Yet all we see on TV are the problems—the unemployment, the suicides, the wounds. Sure, it's a part of who we are, but it isn't the whole story. I believe when our talents, skills, and abilities are leveraged, it will transform this country. I'd change the conversation."

We said our goodbyes and I jumped in my vehicle and headed off to Yellowstone National Park with my wife and two daughters.

As I drove off I wasn't sure if Roger and his team would do anything or if I'd play a role if they did. Rumor had it that the Foundation wanted to do something for veterans, but the veteran space was new to them. Their interests—and funding—had historically been on awareness, community investments and learning innovations that ensured limitless learning for all Idahoans. Simply put, educational initiatives. How veterans would play into this was a bit of a mystery to me.

It wasn't to them.

While I went about the next 15 months moving forward some of our initiatives at our non-profit, the team at Albertsons was doing its homework. It was gathering data points, putting together gaps analyses, and identifying the right partners to put mission above self in order to pull off something big.

The foundation wanted to do something big—but not for fanfare. They wanted it to change Idaho. So they began to put the blueprint together that would create an environment where veterans who wanted to continue to give back and serve had the opportunity to do so.

They were convinced that the skills and attributes veterans possess can have an incredible impact on the communities throughout Idaho.

But in order for it to work, it would take collaboration and collaboration takes time. It would take state government, higher education, private industry, non-profits, and veterans all working together toward one mission.

That one mission today is Mission43—honoring the 43rd State. It is Idaho united with veterans and military families to learn, lead and inspire in their communities.

And it starts with the veteran.

Mission43 is not for all veterans. It is not for those who think they are owed something for their service. Instead, it is for that veteran who wants to give back, who want to lead, who is committed to learning, and who wants to inspire. It is for the veteran who wants to be a part of continuing to make Idaho a great state.

JKAF focused first on creating a blueprint: they would create a network that provides pathways to social connections as well as opportunities to serve in the community in an effort to create a sense of purpose similar to what one felt in the military. They would create partnerships with and trainings for its universities and colleges, so the faculty and staff would better understand the value of veterans as well as how to enable an effective use of the post 9/11 GI Bill; and finally, they would need to provide an effective pathway to making available the resources for a transition into a new career—careers that would benefit not only the veteran, but Idaho as a whole.

Once they had the blueprint, they sought the right partners. Easier said than done. In a world of competing interests and egos, this required some serious work.

They found that, throughout the country, there is a tendency to bring in as many of the great veteran service organizations as one can find. But the challenge with that approach is establishing and managing true collaboration.

So, instead, they evaluated and found the best Veteran Service Organizations in the country that aligned with their focused goal to create social connections, a sense of purpose, better education, and employment opportunities. When they found them, they pulled all four of them together—in one room—and got them to agree that they would help each other and work together so that Mission43 would be a success.

Team RWB (TeamRWB.org), which stands for Team Red, White and Blue, was tasked with connecting veterans to the community through physical and social activities.

Team Rubicon (TeamRubiconUSA.org) was tasked with providing missions with purpose; uniting the skills and experiences of veterans with first responders to rapidly deploy emergency response teams.

Operation Military Family (OMFCares.org) was tasked with taking on the higher educational institutions—providing training to faculty and staff so they have a better understanding of what assets they have in the classroom.

And Hire Heroes USA (HireHeroesUSA.org) is helping solve the employment piece by helping veterans understand how to transform their military service into civilian success.

Each of the organizations is tasked with a specific function within the ecosystem. And each organization committed to joining Mission43 and working together as a team under the assumption that the impact can be much greater when they joined forces.

Once the alliances were made, a leader was needed. So JKAF assumed the leadership role and is providing program oversight and management so there is cohesiveness and assistance in creating opportunities for the organizations to thrive. In addition to leadership, every great initiative requires seed funds. So JKAF is also providing multi-year grants to the participating organizations. But the grant money isn't just given with little expected in return. Key performance indicators and measureable outcomes are established and then JKAF analyzes the performance of the organizations and evaluates their success. For example, a certain number of veterans and spouses must find full-time employment at or above a specified starting salary each year.

Mission43 is just now gaining traction in 2016 and while there are not yet long-term definitive outcomes, there is momentum and excitement throughout the state of Idaho.

The foundation has adopted an attitude of always challenging their assumptions and being very adaptable in how they operate. They are fixed on the mission, but flexible on the method. Of course, that adaptability is being driven by Bryan, a graduate of West Point, Ranger qualified and a veteran of multiple deployments as a helicopter pilot in Iraq and Afghanistan with the 160th Special Operations Aviation Regiment (Nightstalkers). He is managing the details of the initiative.

If there is one key element that is driving the excitement and the early successes, it is having the right people on the team.

Collaboration is the key.

There is no question that education plays a powerful role in how people think and what people choose to do with their lives. America's success or failures rest on the shoulders of its leaders and education is at the foundation of those decisions.

And some of the best education will take place in the state of Idaho because of collaboration.

MENTIONED
RESOURCES

Throughout the book I referenced a few individuals who have written books and a handful of resources. This is by no means an exhaustive list so know that my respect and admiration for other authors and organizations doesn't stop with this list. This is just a start.

But it is a great start and I do I encourage you to check these out.
T*he Suicide Solution* by Frank Selden: The Suicide Solution brings a new perspective to the issues surrounding suicide: the benefits, the harm, and solutions.

Warlord: Broken by War, Saved by Grace, by Ilario Pantano: With the same intensity that sparked the devoted Marine lieutenant and family man to reenlist in the wake of 9/11, Ilario Pantano brings a passionate new perspective to this updated edition of his "vitally important" (New York Post) and controversial memoir. In the newly added Foreword and Afterword that surround his chronicle from the front lines of the Iraq war and the notorious military tribunal that followed his shooting two insurgents in Al Anbar province, Pantano reveals the amazing journey that pulled him out of the despair and darkness of survivors guilt, and healed his psychic wounds: the uplifting story of his spiritual salvation through Jesus Christ.

Hope Unseen by Scotty Smiley: Blindness became Captain Scotty Smiley's journey of supreme testing. As he lay helpless in the hospital, he resented the theft of his dreams—becoming a CEO, a Delta Force operator, or a four-star general. With his wife Tiffany's love and the support of his family and friends, Scotty's response became God's transforming moment. The injury only intensified his indomitable spirit. Since the moment he jumped out of a hospital bed and forced his way through nurses and cords to take a simple shower, Captain Scotty Smiley has climbed Mount Rainier, won an ESPY as Best Outdoor Athlete, surfed, skydived, become a father, earned an MBA from Duke, taught leadership at West Point, commanded an army company, and won the MacArthur Leadership Award. Scotty and Tiffany Smiley have lived out a faith so real that it will inspire you to question your own doubts, push you to serve something bigger than yourself, and encourage you to cling to a Hope Unseen.

The Resilience Trilogy by MG Bob Dees (retired): While troops, veterans, and military families must dig deeply to bounce back from the challenges and trauma of military service, the reality is that all of us need resilience. We are each "warriors" as we battle the trials and tribulations, the body slams of life. We each need the ability to get better and not bitter when the unexplained storms of life assault us, our families and friends, and our very identity. In each of the resilience trilogy books, we address how to "build bounce," how to "weather the storm," and how to "bounce back without getting stuck;" written largely from the context of the military with a rich salting of inspiring stories and valuable spiritual principles.

Operation Military Family: How Military Couples are Fighting to Preserve their Marriages by Michael Schindler: This book covers the 4 stages of a deployment and reveals how couples manage to keep their marriages together through each stage. The book is packed with practical, how-to tips and valuable resources designed to strengthen our warfighter couples.

Team RWB (TeamRWB.org): Their mission is to enrich lives of veterans by connecting them to the community through physical and social activities. They operate in over seven regions, have over 100 members, and host events in over 170 locations.

Hire Heroes USA (HireHeroesUSA.org): They help solve the employment piece by helping veterans understand how to transform their military service into civilian success. HHUSA provides virtual career coaching, transition workshops, interview preparation, and key connections into the civilian workplace.

Team Rubicon (TeamRubiconUSA.org): They provide missions with purpose; uniting the skills and experiences of veterans with first responders to rapidly deploy emergency response teams.

Operation Military Family (OMFCares.org): One of its primary service pillars is equipping communities, which involves training and preparing those who are educating tomorrow's leaders. They provide training and educational workshops for faculty and staff designed to overcome veteran myths and better equip the educator on how to leverage America's greatest asset inside the classroom.

SUMMARY
10 Reasons U.S. Veterans Are America's Greatest Asset

America's greatest asset could be your next door neighbor, the person you pass in the grocery store, a student in your lecture hall, or the person sitting next to you at church. Or it could be you.

Know this, the 7 percent of those who have served this country are ready, willing, and able to step into their next mission: helping American industry, our communities, and our government achieve new heights.

From this book, you were introduced to veterans who displayed GRIT, ADAPTABILITY, and PERSEVERANCE. You also discovered that veterans and their families learn to be SOLUTION-MINDED, and that having OPTIMISM, being LOYAL, leaning on VALUES and showing RESPECT are qualities most veterans bring to the marketplace.

Veterans are GAP SOLVRs. And when America embraces this truth without hesitation, as we did after World War II, she will once again thrive.

One last point, there are 10 things that require zero skill—just dedication—that companies want and our veterans possess or do. The next time you interview a veteran or walk a veteran across your campus on a tour, ask yourself if you see these things:

1. Being on time
2. Work ethic
3. Effort
4. Positive Body language
5. Energy
6. Positive Attitude
7. Passion
8. Being coachable
9. Doing extra
10. Being prepared

ABOUT THE AUTHOR

Michael Schindler, Navy veteran, and CEO of Edmonds-based Operation Military Family, is a guest writer for *Veterans News Now* and author of the books *Operation Military Family* and *U.S. Veterans in the Work Force: Why the 7 Percent are America's Greatest Asset.*

He also writes for one of the longest existing veteran blogs "*The Military Wire.*" He is a popular keynote speaker who reaches thousands of service members and their families every year through workshops and seminars which include "How to Battle-Ready Your Relationship," "What Your Mother-in-Law Didn't Tell You" and "How to Talk Your Way into Better Sex and Make Money From It."

Some of his accomplishments include:

- Outstanding Patriotic Service Award Recipient—WA Department of Veterans Affairs

- Parent Map's "Super Hero for Washington Families" Award

- Amway Corporation's Hero Award for Patriotism

- Executed high level Senate and Pentagon meetings (incl. with Vice Chief of Staff of Army) to discuss merits of transition policies

- Assisted Department of Commerce that assessed defense-sector drawdown preparedness throughout Washington State agencies resulting in the establishment of the Governor's Subcabinet on Military Downsizing

- Helped create the "paperless Veteran" and improved the state's Comp & Pen standing in North Carolina

- Q13 Fox News Military/Veteran Subject Matter Expert – contributor to Seattle's Q13 Fox news on issues related to veterans and military/government-connected issues

To reach Mike Schindler, you can email him at mschindler@opmil-fam.com or call 206-795-5890.

REFERENCES

1   Altman, G. (2015, April 13). *www.militarytimes.com*. Retrieved
     from Military Times: http://www.militarytimes.
     com/story/veterans/
     best-for-vets/2015/04/13/best-for-vets-employers-2015-new-rankings-
     are-out/25704103/

i   Maurer, R. (2015, November 11). Retrieved from Society for Human
     Resource Management: http://www.shrm.org/hrdisciplines/staffingman-
     agement/articles/pages/vets-unemployment-falls-under-national-average.
     aspx

ii   https://reaganlibrary.archives.gov/archives/speeches/1984/82384f.htm

iii Excerpt from "The Suicide Solution" by Frank Selden/reported by Rory
     McCarthy, Wednesday 19 May 2004, The Guardian

iv   Excerpt from The Suicide Solution by Frank Selden

v   http://www.uscarriers.net/lha4history.htm

vi   http://www.uscarriers.net/lha4history.htm

vii https://www.usnwc.edu/About.aspx

viii "The workshop heroes." The Economist. (2013-03-02)

ix   AUTHOR ushistory.org, Operation Desert Storm, U.S. History Online
     Textbook, http://www.ushistory.org/us/60a.asp (Tuesday, May 03,
     2016)

x   https://www.mca-marines.org/leatherneck/2014/07/liberation-fallujah

xi   Made popular by General Mattis who, known for his blunt speaking, stated in a message to the 1st Marine Division in 2003, "Demonstrate to the world there is No Better Friend, No Worse Enemy, than a U.S. Marine."

xii   https://en.wikipedia.org/wiki/Ilario_Pantano.

xiii   http://usacac.army.mil/organizations/cace/wocc/courses/wocs

xiv   http://airforcelive.dodlive.mil/2012/09/air-force-core-values-should-extend-into-our-personal-lives-sept-12-2012/#sthash.teDPU5fK.dpuf

xv   https://www.navy.com/careers/special-operations/seals.html%20-%20ft-training-&-advancement#ft-key-responsibilities

xvi   http://drexelhamilton.com/about-us/leadership-team/lawrence-k-doll/

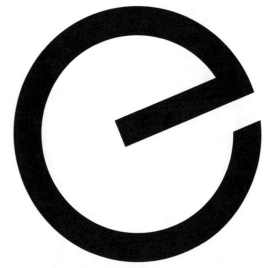

elevate
publishing

DELIVERING TRANSFORMATIVE MESSAGES
TO THE WORLD

Visit www.elevatepub.com for our latest offerings.

NO TREES WERE HARMED IN THE MAKING OF THIS BOOK.

OK, so a few did make the ultimate sacrifice.

In order to steward our environment, we are partnered with *Plant With Purpose,* to plant a tree for every tree that paid the price for the printing of this book.

To learn more, visit www.elevatepub.com/about